Microwave Magic
Fish

Grolier Limited
TORONTO

Contributors to this series:

Recipes and Technical Assistance:
École de cuisine Bachand-Bissonnette
Cooking consultants:
Denis Bissonette
Michèle Émond
Dietician:
Christiane Barbeau
Photos:
Laramée Morel Communications
Audio-Visuelles
Design:
Claudette Taillefer
Assistants:
Julie Deslauriers
Philippe O'Connor
Joan Pothier
Accessories:
Andrée Cournoyer
Writing:
Communications La Griffe Inc.
Text Consultants:
Cap et bc inc.
Advisors:
Roger Aubin
Joseph R. De Varennes
Gaston Lavoie
Kenneth H. Pearson

Assembly:
Carole Garon
Vital Lapalme
Jean-Pierre Larose
Carl Simmons
Gus Soriano
Marc Vallières
Production Managers:
Gilles Chamberland
Ernest Homewood
Production Assistants:
Martine Gingras
Catherine Gordon
Kathy Kishimoto
Peter Thomlison
Art Director:
Bernard Lamy
Editors:
Laurielle Ilacqua
Susan Marshall
Margaret Oliver
Robin Rivers
Lois Rock
Jocelyn Smyth
Donna Thomson
Dolores Williams
Development:
Le Groupe Polygone Éditeurs Inc.

We wish to thank the following firms, PIER I IMPORTS and LE CACHE POT, for their contribution to the illustration of this set.

The series editors have taken every care to ensure that the information given is accurate. However, no cookbook can guarantee the user successful results. The editors cannot accept any responsibility for the results obtained by following the recipes and recommendations given.

Canadian Cataloguing in Publication Data

Main entry under title:

Fish

(Microwave magic ; 5)
Translation of: Le Poisson.
Includes index.
ISBN 0-7172-2426-0

1. Cookery (Fish).   2. Microwave cookery.
I. Series: Microwave magic (Toronto, Ont.) ; 5.

TX832.P6513 1988   641.6'92   C88-094226-6

Contents

Microwave Magic is a multi-volume set, with each volume devoted to a particular type of cooking. So, if you are looking for a chicken recipe, you simply go to one of the two volumes that deal with poultry. Each volume has its own index, and the final volume contains a general index to the complete set.

Microwave Magic puts over twelve hundred recipes at your fingertips. You will find it as useful as the microwave oven itself. Enjoy!

Note from the Editor

How to Use this Book
The books in this set have been designed to make your job as easy as possible. As a result, most of the recipes are set out in a standard way.

We suggest that you begin by consulting the information chart for the recipe you have chosen. You will find there all the information you need to decide if you are able to make it: preparation time, cost per serving, level of difficulty, number of calories per serving and other relevant details. Thus, if you have only 30 minutes in which to prepare the evening meal, you will quickly be able to tell which recipe is possible and suits your schedule.

The list of ingredients is always clearly separated from the main text. When space allows, the ingredients are shown together in a photograph so that you can make sure you have them all without rereading the list—

another way of saving your valuable time. In addition, **for the more complex recipes we have supplied photographs of the key stages involved either in preparation or serving.**

All the dishes in this book have been cooked in a 700 watt microwave oven. If your oven has a different wattage, consult the conversion chart that appears on the following page for cooking times in different types of oven. We would like to emphasize that the cooking times given in the book are a minimum. If a dish does not seem to be cooked enough, you may return it to the oven for a few more minutes. Also, the cooking time can vary according to your ingredients: their water and fat content, thickness, shape and even where they come from. We have therefore left a blank space on each recipe page in which you can note

the cooking time that suits you best. This will enable you to add a personal touch to the recipes that we suggest and to reproduce your best results every time.

Although we have put all the technical information together at the front of this book, we have inserted a number of boxed entries called **MICROTIPS** throughout to explain particular techniques. They are brief and simple, and will help you obtain successful results in your cooking.

With the very first recipe you try, you will discover just how simple microwave cooking can be and how often it depends on techniques you already use for cooking with a conventional oven. If cooking is a pleasure for you, as it is for us, it will be all the more so with a microwave oven. Now let's get on with the food.

The Editor

Key to the Symbols
For ease of reference, the following symbols have been used on the recipe information charts.

The pencil symbol is a reminder to write your cooking time in the space provided.

Level of Difficulty

Easy

Moderate

Complex

Cost per Serving

$ Inexpensive

$ $ Moderate

$ $ $ Expensive

Power Levels

All the recipes in this book have been tested in a 700 watt oven. As there are many microwave ovens on the market with different power levels, and as the names of these levels vary from one manufacturer to another, we have decided to give power levels as a percentage. To adapt the power levels given here, consult the chart opposite and the instruction manual for your oven.

Generally speaking, if you have a 500 watt or 600 watt oven you should increase cooking times by about 30% over those given, depending on the actual length of time required. The shorter the original cooking time, the greater the percentage by which it must be lengthened. The 30% figure is only an average. Consult the chart for detailed information on this topic.

Power Levels

HIGH: 100% - 90%	Vegetables (except boiled potatoes and carrots) Soup Sauce Fruits Browning ground beef Browning dish Popcorn
MEDIUM HIGH: 80% - 70%	Rapid defrosting of precooked dishes Muffins Some cakes Hot dogs
MEDIUM: 60% - 50%	Cooking tender meat Cakes Fish Seafood Eggs Reheating Boiled potatoes and carrots
MEDIUM LOW: 40%	Cooking less tender meat Simmering Melting chocolate
DEFROST: 30% **LOW: 30% - 20%**	Defrosting Simmering Cooking less tender meat
WARM: 10%	Keeping food warm Allowing yeast dough to rise

Cooking Time Conversion Chart

700 watts	600 watts*
5 s	11 s
15 s	20 s
30 s	40 s
45 s	1 min
1 min	1 min 20 s
2 min	2 min 40 s
3 min	4 min
4 min	5 min 20 s
5 min	6 min 40 s
6 min	8 min
7 min	9 min 20 s
8 min	10 min 40 s
9 min	12 min
10 min	13 min 30 s
20 min	26 min 40 s
30 min	40 min
40 min	53 min 40 s
50 min	66 min 40 s
1 h	1 h 20 min

* There is very little difference in cooking times between 500 watt ovens and 600 watt ovens.

The Bountiful Sea

Despite her mysterious and sometimes destructive power, the sea is always bountiful. A symbol of life, the sea provides food, which is as necessary to life as it is prized. Indeed, fish is the second most widely consumed food, the first being grains.

More than twenty thousand different types of fish inhabit the waters of the world's oceans, lakes and rivers, so there is certainly a type of fish to please every palate. The natural habitat of the aquatic creature will affect the way it tastes. For example, saltwater fish are known to be more flavorful than freshwater fish. Also, fish from cold waters generally have a more delicate taste than their warm-water cousins.

For as long as people have been writing about food and cooking—and probably for much longer—cooks have been demonstrating their ingenuity by devising methods of preparing fish that enhance the virtues of the various species. Fish is suited to all cooking methods and can be garnished with various vegetables or condiments; it can be used as a stuffing or a soup base and its trimmings create fragrant stocks. Fish can also be prepared in combination with other ingredients to make a bouillabaisse, a mousseline or a zéphir.

Whether a simple but hearty fish stew prepared on the beach by fishermen back from the sea or an elaborate feast artfully conceived by the most illustrious chefs, fish is a food that is always delicate and delicious.

For a long time limited consumption on days of abstinence, fish deserves a more important place in our diet, where it can contribute to increasing nutritional variety. Fresh, frozen or canned, fish has many nutritional qualities and can play an important role in a well-balanced diet.

The nutritional qualities of fish are significant; fish is easily digested, is rich in protein, contains major quantities of phosphorus, magnesium, copper, iron and Vitamin B and is low in calories. Furthermore, it contains only polyunsaturated fats.

Fish are classified according to whether they are lean, medium fat or fat. Cod, halibut and haddock are lean fish while salmon and mackerel are considered fat fish. However, the fattest fish, the eel, is no more fatty than pork. (See the chart on page 10 for the way in which a number of fish are classified.)

The advent of the microwave oven, as revolutionary as this new technology is, does not dramatically alter the rich tradition of fish cuisine. Of course, the cooking techniques must be adapted to the new microwave, but the cooking principles and, above all the flavor of the fish, remain the same.

This volume of *Microwave Magic,* one of two dedicated to fish and seafood cookery, will demonstrate this point. As well as classifications of the most prized fish and recommendations for choosing and buying fish, you will find an explanation of microwave techniques and more than forty recipes which will serve to convince you that fish is a food of choice both for everyday meals and for special occasions.

Classifications of Fish

Fish	Classification	Method of Cooking	Substitutions
Cod	Lean	All methods*	Goby, haddock, halibut, whiting
Goby	Lean	All methods*	Cod, haddock, halibut, whiting
Haddock	Lean	All methods*	Cod, halibut, whiting, sole
Halibut	Medium fat	All methods*	Cod, haddock, turbot
Herring	Fat	Braised, à l'étuvée	None
Mackerel	Fat	Poached, steamed	Salmon, sturgeon, tuna
Perch	Fat	All methods*	Trout
Pickerel	Lean	All methods*	Trout
Plaice	Lean	Poached, steamed	Haddock, halibut, perch, sole, turbot
Salmon	Fat	All methods*	Mackerel, sturgeon, tuna
Sea perch	Medium fat	Poached, steamed	None
Smelt	Fat	Braised, à l'étuvée	None
Sole	Lean	Poached, steamed	Haddock, halibut, perch, plaice, turbot
Sturgeon	Fat	All methods*	Mackerel, salmon, tuna
Trout	Fat	All methods*	Perch, pickerel
Tuna	Fat	All methods*	Mackerel, salmon, sturgeon
Turbot	Medium	Poached, steamed	Haddock, halibut
Whiting	Lean	All methods*	Cod, goby, haddock, halibut

* Methods include: Poaching, steaming, braising and à l'étuvée (cooked in a covered pan with very little liquid). Note that we have not included non-microwave methods of cooking such as grilling and frying.

10

Recommendations for Buying Fish

Freshness Above All

Indisputably, freshness is the principal criterion for judging the quality of fish. To avoid disappointment at the table, check for the following when buying whole fish:

— the eyes should be bright and rounded (not sunken);
— the gills should be bright red and clean, with no film;
— the scales should be securely attached to the skin;
— the skin should be firm and shiny;
— the smell should be fresh —do not select fish with a strong or unpleasant odor; fresh fish is practically odorless.

When buying fish fillets or steaks, make sure that the flesh is translucent but still retains its color, that it is moist, that it is not brown or discolored in any way and that the edges are not turned up. A dry or milky looking flesh indicates that the fish is no longer fresh. When buying steaks make sure that the bones are firmly implanted in the flesh.

If you are lucky enough to be able to catch your own fish, don't forget to remove the scales as quickly as possible. They contain substances that begin to alter the abdominal wall of the fish the moment it is removed from water.

Fresh or Frozen?

It is not necessary to always use fresh fish in your cooking. Today a wide variety of frozen fish is available commercially. If you choose to use frozen fish, check the water-tightness of the package and make sure there is no sign of prior defrosting. In such a case the flesh would be discolored, brownish or covered with ice crystals. An excessive or extended freezing will produce whitish freezer burn stains which alter the quality of the fish. Generally, frozen products that are vacuum-packed do not present these problems.

Can I Substitute One Type of Fish for Another?

Sometimes after choosing a recipe you may wish to substitute one type of fish for another, depending on availability, seasonality or price, or simply to satisfy your own taste preferences or those of your guests. We have taken this possibility into consideration; for this reason most of the recipes in this volume can be prepared successfully using a kind of fish other than that indicated in the recipe. Consult the chart on page 10 for our recommendations as to the kinds of fish that can be used as substitutes for each other.

A Guide to Freezing Fish

Of course, each type of fish has its own special taste; some gourmets swear by the refined flavor of sole, others favor the delicate taste of haddock. But as the popular expression goes, ''to each his own,'' and there is no reason why you cannot exchange one type of fish for another and adapt the ingredients or the method of preparation to a recipe you enjoy. Just make sure that the two types of fish share some common characteristics, for example, they should:

— be of the same thickness and weight;
— be cut in the same way;
— be in the same category in terms of fatness or leanness.

The latter is especially important because the effect of the microwaves is directly related to the amount of fat contained in the food.
As for recommended quantities per serving and seasonal availability for fish, consult the above charts.

Recommended Quantities (per person)

Whole fish	225 g to 340 g (8 oz to 12 oz)
Trimmed fish (head, tail, fins, entrails and scales removed)	225 g (8 oz)
Fillets, steaks, portions	175 g (6 oz)

Prime Season for Some Popular Fish

Atlantic salmon	May, June, July
Carp	Spring, summer
Cod	Summer
Herring	Spring
Mackerel	Mainly summer
Sea bream	Summer, winter
Smelt	Spring (permanently in some lakes)
Sturgeon	Spring, summer
Trout	All year, depending on the region
Tuna	May to October
Whiting	All year

Preparing Fish

When preparing a whole fish, lay it flat on a cutting board. With very sharp scissors, trim the dorsal fin from the top of the back, then remove the pelvic and ventral fins. To remove the bones easily it is best to remove the dorsal fin completely. To do so, make a deep incision along each side of the full length of the fin, insert a knife under the backbone and remove the fin together with the bones that support it. Then, with a sharp knife, cut off the head and tail.

MICROTIPS

How To Stuff a Whole Fish

After eviscerating and carefully cleaning the fish, dry it with paper towel. Make a deep incision along the underside of the fish from the head to the tail. Half open the fish and sprinkle it with lemon juice. Fill it with the prepared stuffing. With strong white string, tie the fish so that it keeps its shape and the stuffing stays in place.

Scaling Fish

With scissors, cut off the dorsal and other fins so they don't nick you while you are working. To scale a fish easily use a sharp knife or a fish scaler. Lay the fish flat and grasp it firmly by the tail. With the knife or fish scaler scrape off the scales, beginning at the tail and working, against the "nap," toward the head. Repeat the operation two or three times, until the entire surface is free of scales.

Turn the fish over and remove the scales from the other side. The area around the head and the base of the fins can be a little more difficult to scale perfectly. You may have to repeat the operation more than two or three times. To avoid making a mess with the scales and to make the process easier, try immersing the fish in a basin of cold water before scaling it.

Complete this procedure by rinsing the scaled fish in cold water and patting it dry.

Eviscerating Fish

Fish can be eviscerated from the stomach or from the gills. If the recipe requires that the head be removed, cut it off just behind the gills with a sharp knife.

With a strong knife cut along the entire length of the belly of the fish from the head to the vent and remove the entrails. Cut along the backbone (from the underside) to loosen any remaining coagulated blood.

Complete the procedure by rinsing the fish thoroughly in cold water and patting it dry.

Skinning Fish

 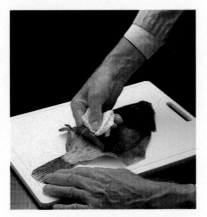 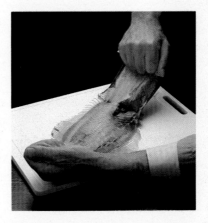

Some types of fish, such as sole or halibut, should be skinned before being prepared. Removing the skin of the fish is easily done.

Lay the fish flat on a chopping board, placing the darker side up. With a sharp knife make an incision through the skin at the base of the tail. Slide the point of the knife in between the flesh and the skin, carefully detaching one from the other. Grasp the released skin firmly with a cloth and begin to pull it back.

Holding the tail flat and taut with the other hand, continue to pull the skin steadily from the tail toward the head. The skin should come away in one piece without ripping. Turn the fish over and repeat the operation.

MICROTIPS

Sharpening Knives: A Delicate But Indispensable Task

To protect your knives and to facilitate your use of them it is necessary to sharpen them regularly. Remember that a dull knife is not only difficult to use, it can also be dangerous. For this reason it is very useful to have a knife sharpener, known as a steel. Electric knife sharpeners are not recommended because they wear down the blade prematurely.

To sharpen knives, first hold the sharpener (the steel) firmly by the handle. With the other hand lay the heel of the blade against the tip of the steel at an angle of 15° to 25°, drawing the blade down toward the base of the steel until it reaches the safety edge. Use a quick swinging motion of the wrist for each stroke. Repeat this procedure, alternating the sides of the blade against the steel, about 10 times.

We strongly suggest that you sharpen your knives regularly, after 2 or 3 uses. For maintenance, we recommend that you rinse the knife in warm water and dry it after each use; avoid the dishwasher. Check the sharpness of a knife by trying to cut a tomato without squishing it.

Filleting Fish

To remove fish fillets use a knife with a long, thin, flexible blade. The method we describe here can be applied to most types of fish.

Lay the fish flat so that the dorsal fin faces the hand holding the knife.

Make two incisions along each side of the dorsal fin from head to tail. Insert the point of the knife between the flesh and the fin and cut along the backbone, as shown, deep enough to expose the backbone.

Lay the fish on its side and detach the flesh from behind the gills by carefully sliding the point of the knife between the flesh and the fins.

Holding the blade of the knife flat, slide it along the ribs, from head to tail, detaching the fillet so that it comes off in one piece. Retain the dorsal fin and remove the fillet on the other side in the same way.

To remove the skin, lay the fillet, skin-side down, and cut through the flesh about 1 cm (1/2 inch) above the tail. Hold the tail firmly and work the knife along at a shallow angle against the skin, cutting the flesh free.

The fillet, located lengthwise along the fish below its dorsal fin, is undoubtedly the most prized and most widely used part of the fish. Poached, steamed or prepared with a sauce, the fillet is always appreciated. Most types of fish can be filleted, but this cut is especially well suited to fish with a well-defined bone structure. Most fish have two fillets, but some fish belonging to the category of flat fish have a double set; when skinned an indentation down the center of each side reveals two fillets on each side.

Many people don't eat fish simply because they find eating the small bones disagreeable. However, the bones can easily be removed to overcome this problem. There are two methods of doing this. Filleting the fish eliminates almost all the

Boning Whole Fish

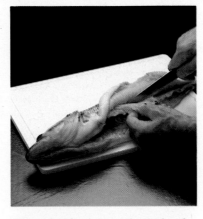

Cut along the entire length of the belly of the fish, from head to tail, and remove the viscera. Rinse in cold water. Trim the fish by removing the dorsal fins and the bones that support it, as well as the pectoral and pelvic fins.

Run a knife along either side of the backbone to release any blood pockets. Rinse well in cold water again.

Lay the fish flat and open it to expose the lateral bones, or the ribs, attached to the backbone. The ribs are covered by a thin membrane which must be pierced to remove them.

Working along the fish, carefully pierce the membrane to expose each rib. Slide the knife blade under each rib to lift it free of the flesh and detach from the backbone. Spread the fish open and separate the backbone from the flesh with sharp knife.

Sever the backbone as close to the head as possible. Grasp the severed end and lift carefully, freeing the backbone from the flesh. Do not tear or damage the flesh.

The bones of the fish should be kept to make fish stock.

bones. This method applies to recipes using fillets of fish.

The other way of proceeding is to bone the whole fish, a method obviously suited to recipes requiring the presentation of a whole fish.

Most fish have a bone structure formed by a backbone attached to several lateral bones, or ribs. These bones are easily removed by slitting the fish along the underside, from head to tail, removing the viscera and

opening the fish to remove the bones. A detailed description of this procedure is given above.

Preparing Fish Steaks

 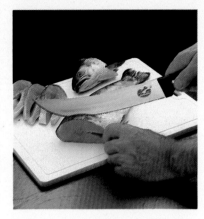 

Fish that are too large to be filleted or cooked whole in the microwave oven are best sliced into steaks. Most often used for salmon and haddock, this cut is one of the easiest to execute, but you must use a very sharp knife or saw; only these utensils will cut through the backbone of the fish. Lay the cleaned fish flat on a chopping board. With a sharp cleaver or saw cut off the head, just behind the gills. Keep the fish head to make a stock.

Keeping the fish flat, cut it vertically into steaks of equal size, at least 2-1/2 cm (1 inch) thick. Steaks cut any thinner would have a tendency to dry out during cooking.

Remove and discard the tail.

Note that with the exception of turbot and halibut, only round fish are cut into steaks. The fish selected must also be large enough to provide practical, serving-sized steaks and should have firm flesh that will not fall apart during cooking. Consult the chart below for guidelines as to the way in which different types of fish should be cut for presentation.

Recommended Cuts for Presentation According to Type of Fish

Type	Presentation	Type	Presentation
Burbot	Whole, fillets	Pike	Whole
Cod	Whole, steaks, fillets	Salmon	Whole, steaks
Haddock	Fillets	Sea perch	Fillets
Herring	Whole	Smelt	Fillets, steaks
Mackerel	Whole, fillets	Sole	Fillets
Mullet	Whole	Trout	Whole
Norway haddock	Fillets	Tuna	Steaks
Perch	Whole, fillets	Yellow perch	Fillets
Pickerel	Whole, fillets		

Salmon

Salmon steaks

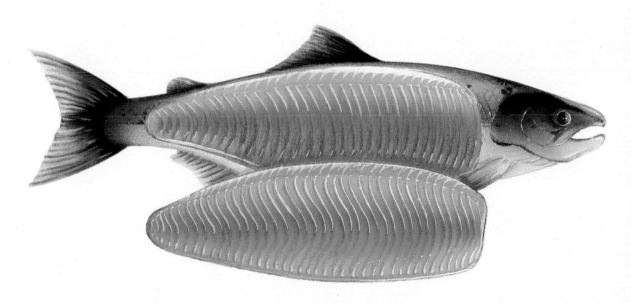

Salmon fillets

19

Freezing Fish

For those who catch their own fish, freezing is a way of prolonging the pleasures of the summer season. Freezing also gives the average consumer the opportunity to take advantage of low-priced fresh consignments at the fish market and is an easy way of always having a quick supper on hand. Any fish to be frozen should first be carefully cleaned. If freezing a whole fish, it is essential that the scales be removed (see page 14).

To prevent any alteration in the quality of the fish, it should be tightly covered with wrapping that is both air- and watertight or with aluminum foil. The best method is to vacuum pack the fish with a special apparatus. Fish will keep best if it is moist when frozen; it is for this reason that it should be frozen as quickly as possible after it is caught or purchased. Naturally, you should label the package with the date of freezing and the name of the fish.

An excellent method of freezing large whole fish is to put the prepared fish on a platter in the freezer for 2 to 3 hours. When the fish is rigid, plunge it into a container of very cold water and then place it in the freezer again. Repeat this procedure 3 or 4 times, laying the fish flat on alternate sides. When the fish is covered with a 5 to 6 mm (about 1/4 inch) layer of ice, wrap it as previously described. This method is not essential, but it does ensure that large fish are properly frozen.

To freeze fish steaks or fillets, separate them carefully with a layer of waxed paper or freezer wrap. Cover them with plastic or freezer wrap to seal in the moisture. By separating the pieces before freezing, they will retain all their texture when defrosted and cooked.

Consult the chart below for recommended freezing times for fat, medium fat and lean fish.

Guide to Freezing Fish

Fat fish: herring, mackerel, perch, salmon, smelt, sturgeon, trout, tuna	3 months
Medium fat fish: halibut, Norway haddock, turbot	4 months
Lean fish: cod, goby, haddock, pickerel, plaice, whiting	6 months

Defrosting Fish

Remove the fish from its wrapping and place it in the center of a rack. Calculate the defrosting time using the directions given in the chart at the bottom of the page, according to the weight of the fish.

Defrost for half the time indicated and then cover the head and tail with aluminum foil to prevent them from cooking prematurely.

Turn the fish over and give the rack a half-turn to ensure even defrosting.

Defrosting Fish Fillets

Fillets	Power Level	Defrosting Time
Block-frozen	30%	13 to 22 min/kg (6 to 10 min/lb)
Individual fillets	30%	11 to 17 min/kg (5 to 8 min/lb)

Upon completion of the defrosting cycle, the fish should be flexible but still cold in the center. Allow a standing time equal to a third of the total defrosting time before proceeding with the recipe so that the defrosting process is complete.

Defrosting Whole Fish

Size	Power Level	Defrosting Time
Small	30%	7 to 15 min/kg (3 to 7 min/lb)
Medium	30%	11 to 17 min/kg (5 to 8 min/lb)
Large	30%	13 to 22 min/kg (6 to 10 min/lb)

Defrosting Fish Steaks

Remove the fish steaks from the freezer and check the exact weight of the fish before beginning the defrosting cycle. Use a microwave-safe rack and set the power level at 30%.

Unwrap the fish steaks without detaching them from the paper used to separate them. Place them in the center of the rack. Calculate the defrosting time at 13 to 22 min/kg (6 to 10 min/lb). Set the oven for half the required time and begin.

Separate the fish steaks, removing the sheets of paper between, and turn them over. Continue the defrosting cycle until all the steaks are flexible but still cold in the center. Let stand for 10 minutes before beginning the recipe so that the defrosting process is complete.

Defrosting Fish Fillets

Remove the fillets from their wrapping and place them in the center of a microwave-safe rack. Set the power level at 30% and check the exact weight of the fish before beginning the defrosting cycle. Calculate the time required from the directions given in the chart on page 21. Set the oven for half the required time and begin.

At the end of the first defrosting period separate the fillets and turn them over. Cover the ends with aluminum foil so that the thinner parts do not begin to cook. Continue defrosting at 30%.

At the end of the second defrosting time the fillets should be flexible but still cold in the center. Allow a standing time equal to one third of the total defrosting time before beginning the recipe so that the defrosting process is complete.

Cooking Fish: Methods

Poaching or Steaming

Poached or steamed, fish will retain all its delicacy and flavor. These methods of cooking are simple but require some attention. Poaching consists of cooking the fish completely immersed in liquid (water, milk or court-bouillon); the volume of liquid varies according to the size of the fish or cuts of fish. Poaching is done over low heat; the liquid should not come to a boil. Steaming consists of placing the food over, not in, a boiling liquid. In both cases, the fish is cooked covered and its fleshy side should be placed toward the outside of the dish.

Cooking *à l'étuvée*

The advantage of this method of cooking is that the fish is cooked mainly in its own liquid; it is cooked covered with very little additional liquid and with aromatics and vegetables to enhance its flavor. A constant self-basting action takes place as steam condenses and falls back on the food. This method can be used with all types of fish.

Open cooking

Open cooking is a way of grilling the fish in the microwave oven by placing it on a bacon rack. The results are as successful as in a traditional oven. This method is particularly well-suited to fillets of fish. More than with any other method, it is important not to overcook the fish since its naturally tender flesh will dry out.

MICROTIPS

Cook Fish Carefully To Retain Its Delicate Flavor

Methods used to cook fish are generally simple; their principal aim is to preserve all the delicate and nutritional qualities of the fish. Even though the cooking methods used for fish, and most other seafood, are similar to those used for meat, it is important to remember that fish is naturally more tender and requires a shorter cooking time. This characteristic is particularly important in terms of microwave cooking.

For this reason we suggest that you check for doneness, regardless of the cooking method used, periodically during the cooking times given in the charts and recipes in this volume. It is better to check for doneness before the end of the cooking cycle and continue cooking if necessary than to serve overcooked, dried out fish, which has lost all its nutritional value and its delicate flavor.

Of course, this suggestion applies to any type of dish, whether it be meat, vegetables or fish, but since the latter requires a very short cooking time, one minute of overcooking is sufficient to compromise the success of even the best fish recipe.

Cooking Fish: Principles

Fish can be cooked in the microwave oven to satisfy everyone's taste. Whether you use fresh or frozen fish, if properly cooked, the taste will be exceptional and the flesh will be tender and creamy. In fact, microwave cooking produces such spectacular results with fish that you will quickly abandon traditional oven recipes. The microwave oven allows foods to be cooked in very small amounts of liquid and cooking fish in its own natural juices is a method that produces the most flavorful results. The microwaves ensure a perfectly cooked fish which retains all its flavor.

Due to its very delicate flesh, fish should not be overcooked or it will become dry. Check the fish regularly as it cooks. Remember that fish is properly cooked when its flesh can be flaked with a fork. Even if the center of the fish appears transluscent at the end of the required cooking time, the cooking process will continue during the standing time, which must be scrupulously adhered to.

Consult the table above for the recommended cooking times for different cuts of fish.

Cooking Times for Fish

Cut of Fish	Power Level	Cooking Time	Recommendations
Whole	70%	13 to 20 min/kg (6 to 9 min/lb)	Cover the head and tail with aluminum foil during the cooking time.
Steaks	70%	15 to 20 min/kg (7 to 9 min/lb)	Cook until the flesh is easily flaked with a fork.
Fillets	100%	7 to 13 min/kg (3 to 6 minlb)	Cook just until the flesh is easily flaked with a fork.

MICROTIPS

Microwaves and Liquids

Among the many factors that determine the effect of microwaves on foods (thickness, density, weight, sugar and fat content, arrangement during cooking time, etc.), the quantity of liquid is one of the most important. In fact the natural water content of the food and the liquid required to prepare a particular recipe are directly related to the power level, cooking time and cooking method suggested. As a general rule, the higher the water content and the more liquid added, the slower the effect of the microwaves and thus the longer the cooking time.

Dishes for Microwave Cooking

If you have recently acquired a microwave oven, don't rush out to buy a whole new set of dishes and utensils. Your kitchen cupboards are probably filled with dishes that are perfectly suitable for microwave cooking.

All materials that allow microwaves to pass through can be used: glass, paper, earthenware, porcelain (with no metal rim), ceramic containers or straw or wicker baskets. As you can see, the list is a long one. Some dishes are more frequently used than others for cooking fish.

Bacon Rack
Because of its ridged base,

which keeps the food raised and allows the cooking juices to drain away, the bacon rack is particularly well suited to cooking fish.

Covered Dish
Many recipes recommend the use of a dish with a cover. Cooking foods in a covered dish will retain all the moisture during the cooking cycle.

Casserole
A deep casserole is required for simmering fish, for preparing recipes requiring large amounts of liquid ingredients or for preparing large fish.

Platter
A platter is often used to cook small fish or to prepare recipes requiring few ingredients.

MICROTIPS

Microwaves and Metal Do Not Mix!

There are few restrictions in using the microwave oven. One of the few, however, and the most important, is **never to use a dish or container made out of** metal. Remember to check for metal rims and decorations. Also check for metal strips in the ties used to close bags before defrosting or cooking foods in the microwave and replace with microwave-safe ties.

Aromatics, Spices and Condiments for Fish

Among the many elements that enter into the preparation of a recipe, aromatics, spices and condiments are often considered to be less important than the basic ingredients. These elements, however, do play an important role in culinary art because they can enhance a delicate flavor or perfectly effect the combination of diverse flavors.

Fish is a food that must be very carefully seasoned because of its delicate taste. The quantities of aromatic, spices and condiments indicated in a recipe must be adhered to strictly.

Aromatics are distinguished from condiments in that aromatics are used during the culinary preparation process to enhance the flavor or fragrance, to make sweeter, more acidic, saltier or to add fat. When these same substances are added to the dish at the table they are called condiments.

Aromatics are classified according to their dominant flavor.
Sweet Aromatics: bay leaf, juniper, rosemary, chervil, fennel, tarragon, basil, sage, parsley, aniseed, savory, mint, thyme, marjoram.
Pungent Aromatics: cumin, coriander, saffron, pepper, cinnamon, cloves, nutmeg.

Condiments are classified in a more complex manner.
Acidic Condiments: vinegar, verjuice, lemon juice, etc.

Pungent Condiments: garlic, shallots, scallions, chives, onions, mustard, horseradish.
Pungent and Aromatic Condiments: lemon or orange zest, cocoa, coffee, pepper, paprika, pimento, ginger.
Oily Condiments: oils, butter, fat.
Mixed Condiments: prepared English sauces (for example, Worcestershire), ketchup, curry, combination mustards, soy sauce, etc.

Aromatic flavoring agents used in court bouillon, the liquid in which fish is most frequently poached, include carrots, onions, celery, white wine or lemon juice, thyme, bay leaves and parsley.

Two of the most common sauces served with fish include the savory *sabayon* and *beurre blanc.* The former, a close relative of hollandaise, is a blend of butter, egg yolks and fish stock and is frequently flavored with lemon juice and tarragon. The latter combines white wine and butter and is flavored with shallots—a wonderful addition to any sauce for fish.

As well, a number of herbs and spices, used in varying combinations and with a light touch, may be added to sauces for fish. Thyme, basil, chives, chervil, marjoram, pepper, dill and tarragon all enhance the flavor of fish very nicely. And without sauce, a sprinkle of lemon juice, a little grated zest and a touch of any of the above seasonings makes fish absolutely perfect.

Whole Salmon Stuffed with Shrimp

Level of Difficulty	🍴
Preparation Time	20 min
Cost per Serving	$ $ $
Number of Servings	8
Nutritional Value	564 calories 62.1 g protein 31.5 g lipids
Food Exchanges	5 oz meat 2 fat exchanges
Cooking Time	20 min
Standing Time	4 min
Power Level	100%, 70%
Write Your Cooking Time Here	

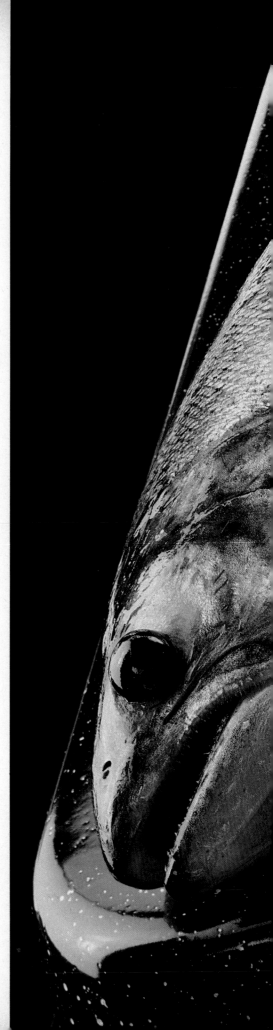

Ingredients
1 whole salmon, 1.8 kg (4 lb)
60 mL (4 tablespoons) butter, melted
125 mL (1/2 cup) Italian breadcrumbs
900 g (2 lb) shrimps, coarsely chopped
zest of 1 lemon
2 eggs, lightly beaten
salt and pepper to taste
2 mL (1/2 teaspoon) tarragon
juice of 1 lemon, or more

Method
— Combine the melted butter, breadcrumbs, shrimps, lemon zest, eggs and seasonings. Mix well.
— Stuff the salmon with this mixture and secure it with string.
— Put the stuffed salmon in a microwave-safe dish.
— Sprinkle with lemon juice.
— Cook at 100% for 2 minutes.
— Reduce the power level to 70% and cook for 8 minutes.
— Turn the salmon over and give the dish a half-turn.
— Continue cooking at 70% for 8 to 10 minutes or until the salmon is almost cooked.
— Let stand for 4 minutes before serving.

Note: This dish can be served with fennel sauce.

Salmon Pie

Level of Difficulty	
Preparation Time	15 min
Cost per Serving	$ $
Number of Servings	4
Nutritional Value	517 calories 26.3 g protein 31.4 g lipids
Food Exchanges	3 oz meat 2 bread exchanges 3 fat exchanges
Cooking Time	10 min
Standing Time	None
Power Level	100%, 70%
Write Your Cooking Time Here	

Ingredients
1 426 mL (15 oz) can salmon
50 mL (1/4 cup) onions,
finely chopped
125 mL (1/2 cup) celery,
finely chopped
50 mL (1/4 cup) green pepper,
diced
125 mL (1/2 cup) sour cream
30 mL (2 tablespoons) red
pepper, cooked and diced
parsley, chopped
5 mL (1 teaspoon) dill
30 mL (1 oz) lemon juice
salt and pepper to taste
1 pie shell, cooked
5 pieces of baked pie dough,
cut in fish shapes

Method
— Drain the salmon and
  remove the skin and
  bones.
— Flake the salmon flesh into
  pieces.
— Combine the onions,
  celery and green peppers.
  Cover and cook at 50%
  for 3 to 4 minutes.
— Add the salmon, sour
  cream, red pepper,
  parsley, dill, lemon juice,
  salt and pepper. Mix well.
— Pour this mixture into the
  pie shell.
— Decorate with the
  fish-shaped pieces of
  pastry.
— Cook on a raised rack at
  70% for 3 minutes.
— Give the dish a half-turn.
  Continue cooking for 2 to
  3 minutes or until the dish
  is very hot.

Clean and drain the salmon before removing the skin.

Combine all the ingredients and pour the mixture into the pie shell.

MICROTIPS

Storing Fresh Fish

Whether whole or cut into steaks or fillets, fish bought fresh will keep for only one day in the refrigerator. It is very important to wrap the fish carefully and store it in the coldest part of the refrigerator.

Salmon Steaks with Duxelles

Level of Difficulty	🍴🍴🍴
Preparation Time	10 min
Cost per Serving	$ $
Number of Servings	4
Nutritional Value	491 calories 39.3 g protein 34.3 g lipids
Food Exchanges	5 oz meat 1/2 vegetable exchange 2 fat exchanges
Cooking Time	8 min
Standing Time	2 min
Power Level	70%
Write Your Cooking Time Here	

Ingredients
4 salmon steaks, 675 g
(1-1/2 lb) in total and 2.5 cm
(1 in) thick
50 mL (1/4 cup) butter
15 mL (1 tablespoon) dried
parsley
50 mL (1/4 cup) green onions,
chopped
250 ml (1 cup) mushrooms,
finely chopped
30 mL (2 tablespoons) lemon
juice
15 mL (1 tablespoon) dried
dill
salt and pepper to taste

Method
— Dry the steaks carefully.
— Melt the butter; add the
  parsley, green onions,
  mushrooms, lemon juice
  and seasonings. Mix well.
— Pour half this mixture into
  a dish and spread it out
  evenly.
— Arrange the salmon steaks
  on top and cover them
  with the remainder of the
  mixture.
— Cover and cook at 70%
  for 4 minutes.
— Move the steaks from the
  center of the dish toward
  the outside and vice versa.
  Continue cooking at 70%
  for 3 to 4 minutes or until
  the steaks are done.
— Let stand for 2 minutes.

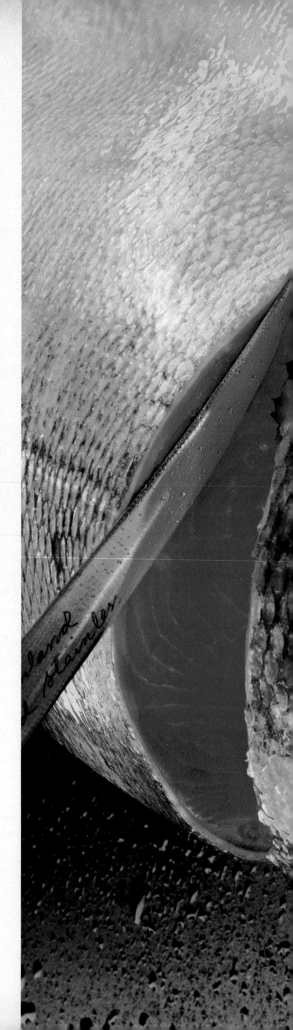

Salmon Manicotti

Level of Difficulty	 (utensils icon)
Preparation Time	30 min
Cost per Serving	$
Number of Servings	4
Nutritional Value	275 calories 21.2 g protein 21 g lipids
Food Exchanges	2.5 oz meat 1 bread exchange
Cooking Time	13 min
Standing Time	2 min
Power Level	100%, 70%
Write Your Cooking Time Here	

Ingredients
1 213 mL (7-1/2 oz) can salmon
125 mL (1/2 cup) cream of celery soup
75 mL (1/3 cup) plain yoghurt
15 mL (1 tablespoon) parsley, chopped
15 mL (1 tablespoon) butter
30 mL (2 tablespoons) onion, finely chopped
1 clove garlic, finely chopped
125 mL (1/2 cup) spinach
150 mL (2/3 cup) cottage cheese
2 mL (1/2 teaspoon) basil
salt and pepper to taste
4 manicotti, cooked *al dente*
Parmesan cheese, grated

Method
— Drain the salmon and set the liquid aside. Remove the skin.
— Combine the salmon, its liquid, the cream of celery soup, yoghurt and parsley, to make a sauce. Set aside.
— Melt the butter at 100% for 40 seconds.
— Add the onions and the garlic; cover and cook at 100% for 2 minutes. Set aside.
— Wash and drain the spinach.
— Cover and cook at 100% for 2 to 3 minutes; drain again through a sieve.
— Combine the spinach and the cottage cheese with the garlic and onion mixture.
— Season with basil, salt and pepper.
— Fill each manicotti with a quarter of the mixture; arrange them on a microwave-safe dish.
— Pour the salmon sauce over the manicotti; sprinkle with Parmesan.
— Cover and cook at 70% for 4 minutes.
— Move the manicotti from the center of the dish to the outside and vice-versa.
— Continue cooking at 70% for 3 minutes or until the mixture is hot.
— Let stand for 2 minutes.

The list of ingredients may seem long, but this delicious recipe can be prepared in only 30 minutes!

Fill each manicotti with a quarter of the mixture of spinach, cottage cheese, garlic and onions.

Pour the salmon sauce over the manicotti and sprinkle with Parmesan before cooking in a covered dish.

Salmon Ring Loaf

Level of Difficulty	🍴
Preparation Time	15 min
Cost per Serving	**$**
Number of Servings	4
Nutritional Value	250 calories 26 g protein 12.6 g lipids
Food Exchanges	3.5 oz meat 1/2 vegetable exchange 1/2 fat exchange
Cooking Time	9 min
Standing Time	3 min
Power Level	70%
Write Your Cooking Time Here	

Ingredients
1 426 mL (15 oz) can salmon
125 mL (1/2 cup) onion
croutons
125 mL (1/2 cup) celery,
finely chopped
50 mL (1/4 cup) green pepper,
finely chopped
2 eggs, lightly beaten
50 mL (1/4 cup) sour cream
salt and pepper to taste
several strips of red pepper,
cooked
2 mL (1/2 teaspoon) lemon
zest

Method
— Drain the salmon and
remove the bones and
skin. Flake the salmon
and add the croutons,
celery, green pepper, eggs,
sour cream and the
seasonings; mix well.
— Grease the inside of a
microwave-safe ring dish.
— Arrange the strips of
cooked red pepper
decoratively in the bottom
of the dish.
— Carefully pour the salmon
mixture into the pan.
Press down with the palm
of your hand.
— Cover and cook on a
raised rack at 70% for 4
minutes.
— Give the dish a half-turn
and continue cooking at
70% for 4 to 5 minutes or
until cooked; check for
doneness with a
toothpick.
— Let stand for 3 minutes;
garnish with the lemon
zest before serving.

Combine the main ingredients and pour into a greased pan. Cook on a raised rack.

Check for doneness with a toothpick; the mixture is cooked if the toothpick comes away clean.

MICROTIPS

Ring Dishes

Ring dishes are wonderful for the even cooking of meat or fish loaves in the microwave oven as there is no food in the center, where the microwaves are least intense. But if you don't have one, use an ordinary microwave-safe bowl with an upside-down glass placed in the center of the bowl.

Trout *au bleu*

Level of Difficulty	🍴
Preparation Time	5 min
Cost per Serving	$ $
Number of Servings	4
Nutritional Value	304 calories 31.5 g protein 17.3 g lipids
Food Exchanges	4 oz meat
Cooking Time	20 min
Standing Time	10-15 min
Power Level	100%
Write Your Cooking Time Here	

Ingredients
4 whole trout, 340 g (12 oz) each
250 mL (1 cup) hot water
juice of 1 lemon
2 celery stalks, sliced
1 large carrot, cubed
1 medium onion, cut in two
4 sprigs fresh parsley
5 mL (1 teaspoon) tarragon
2 bay leaves
10 peppercorns
250 mL (1 cup) tarragon-flavored wine vinegar
watercress and lemon quarters to garnish

Method
— Pour the water, lemon juice, celery, carrot, onion, parsley and tarragon into a large microwave-safe dish.
— Cover and cook at 100% for 10 to 12 minutes, or until the carrots are cooked.
— Strain everything through a sieve and press well to extract as much liquid as possible.
— Pour the liquid back into the dish; add the bay leaf, peppercorns and vinegar.
— Cover and cook at 100% until boiling.
— Carefully place the trout in the casserole; cover and cook at 100% for 5 minutes.
— Leave in the liquid and let stand, covered, for 10 to 15 minutes.
— Carefully remove the trout and place on a paper towel to dry.
— Garnish with watercress and lemon quarters before serving.

MICROTIPS

Seafood-Based Prepared Butters

Some seafood can be used to make such prepared butters as anchovy, crab or shrimp butter. Anchovy butter is served with grilled fish or meat and is easy to prepare. You need only 115 grams (4 oz) of butter and 6 anchovy fillets. First rinse the anchovies in cold water, dry them well and chop. Push them through a strainer and mix well with the butter.

For crab or shrimp butters, combine equal parts of butter and crab or shrimp meat, passed through a sieve.

Trout with Sour Cream

Level of Difficulty	🍴
Preparation Time	15 min
Cost per Serving	$ $
Number of Servings	4
Nutritional Value	391 calories 31.8 g protein 10.3 g lipids
Food Exchanges	4 oz meat 1/2 bread exchange 2 fat exchanges
Cooking Time	12 min
Standing Time	None
Power Level	100%, 70%
Write Your Cooking Time Here	

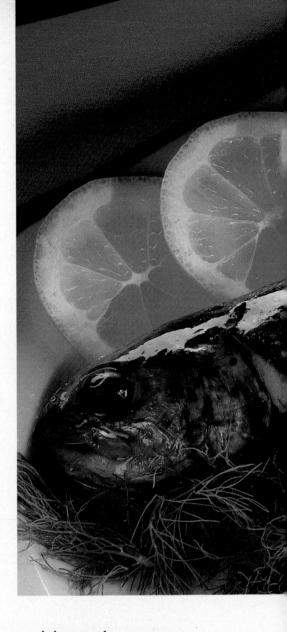

Ingredients
4 whole trout
salt and pepper to taste
50 mL (1/4 cup) breadcrumbs
15 mL (1 tablespoon) oil
30 mL (2 tablespoons) butter
15 mL (1 teaspoon) onion, finely chopped
50 mL (1/4 cup) lemon juice
15 mL (1 tablespoon) parsley, chopped
2 mL (1/2 teaspoon) tarragon
75 mL (1/3 cup) sour cream

Method
— Wash the trout and pat with a damp cloth.
— Season the cavities with salt and pepper.
— Preheat a browning dish at 100% for 7 minutes. Coat the trout with breadcrumbs.
— Pour the oil and butter into the browning dish; heat at 100% for 30 seconds.
— Sear the trout and remove immediately. Set aside.
— Heat the dish again at 100% for 40 seconds.
— Add the onion, lemon juice, parsley, tarragon and sour cream; mix well.
— Heat at 100% for 2 minutes.
— Put the trout in the dish; cover and cook at 70% for 4 minutes.
— Move the trout from the center of the dish toward the outside and vice versa.
— Cook at 70% for 4 to 6 minutes or until the trout are cooked.

Pat the trout carefully with a damp cloth before cooking.

Sear the trout in a preheated browning dish; set aside and continue with the recipe.

MICROTIPS

To Sear Fish
Preheat a browning dish at 100% for 7 minutes. Since the dish becomes very hot, protect your hands when taking it out of the oven. Add butter or oil and heat at 100% for 30 seconds. Then sear the fish in the browning dish and watch out for splattering.

Stuffed Fillets of Sole

Level of Difficulty	🍴
Preparation Time	20 min
Cost per Serving	$ $
Number of Servings	4
Nutritional Value	394 calories 43.8 g protein 16.5 g lipids
Food Exchanges	4.5 oz meat 1/4 bread exchange 5 fat exchanges
Cooking Time	14 min
Standing Time	None
Power Level	100%, 70%
Write Your Cooking Time Here	

Ingredients

900 g (2 lb) sole fillets
60 mL (4 tablespoons) butter
1 clove garlic
175 mL (3/4 cup) small
shrimps
50 mL (1/4 cup) crackers,
crushed
salt and pepper to taste
125 mL (1/2 cup) hot chicken
bouillon
125 mL (1/2 cup) white wine
45 mL (3 tablespoons) butter,
cut in cubes
30 mL (2 tablespoons)
cornstarch
50 mL (1/4 cup) cold milk
15 mL (1 tablespoon) fresh
parsley, chopped

Method

— Combine the butter, garlic
  and shrimp in a bowl;
  cover and cook at 100%
  for 2 to 3 minutes.
— Add the cracker crumbs,
  salt and pepper; mix well.
— Wash and pat the sole
  fillets dry.
— Spread the stuffing over
  the fillets; roll up and
  secure with toothpicks.
— Arrange the rolled fillets in
  a microwave-safe dish.
— Add the hot chicken
  bouillon and the wine.
— Place a cube of butter on
  each fillet.
— Cover the dish with plastic
  wrap, leaving one corner
  open for the steam to
  escape.

⟹

Stuffed Fillets of Sole

Assemble all the ingredients required to prepare this recipe.

After washing the fillets, pat them carefully with a damp cloth.

Spread each fillet with the stuffing, roll up and secure with toothpicks.

Arrange the fillets in a microwave-safe dish, add the bouillon and wine and place a cube of butter on each.

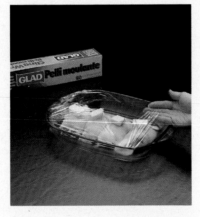

Cover the dish with plastic wrap, leaving one corner open to allow for the escape of steam.

Cook the fillets, set aside and reserve 250 mL (1 cup) of the cooking liquid.

— Cook at 70% for 4 minutes.
— Move the fillets from the center of the dish to the outside and vice versa.
— Cook at 70% for 4 minutes or until the fillets are cooked.

— Drain the fillets and reserve 250 mL (1 cup) of the cooking liquid.
— Dissolve the cornstarch in the cold milk.
— Add the milk and the parsley to the cooking liquid, whisking

vigorously.
— Cook at 100% for 2 to 3 minutes or until the sauce thickens, stirring each minute.
— Pour the sauce over the fillets and serve.

Fillets of Sole with Almonds

Ingredients
450 g (1 lb) sole fillets
75 mL (1/3 cup) butter, melted
125 mL (1/2 cup) slivered almonds
2 mL (1/2 teaspoon) salt
1 mL (1/4 teaspoon) white pepper
10 mL (2 teaspoons) parsley, chopped
15 mL (1 tablespoon) lemon juice

Level of Difficulty	🍴
Preparation Time	5 min
Cost per Serving	$
Number of Servings	4
Nutritional Value	319 calories 20.3 g protein 25.5 g lipids
Food Exchanges	3 oz meat 3 fat exchanges
Cooking Time	8 min
Standing Time	2 min
Power Level	100%, 90%
Write Your Cooking Time Here	✏️🍎

Method
— Melt the butter at 100% for 1 minute; add the almonds.
— Cook at 100% for 3 to 4 minutes or until the almonds are golden, stirring after 2 minutes.
— Remove the almonds and set them aside.
— Arrange the fillets in a dish, with the fleshy parts toward the outside.
— Pour the butter over the fillets; season with the salt, pepper, parsley and lemon juice.
— Cover and cook at 90% for 2 minutes.
— Give the dish a half-turn; cook at 90% for 2 minutes longer or until the fillets are cooked.
— Garnish with the almonds; cover and let stand for 2 minutes.

Fillets of Sole Breaded Italian Style

Level of Difficulty	 (fork/knife symbol)
Preparation Time	5 min
Cost per Serving	$
Number of Servings	4
Nutritional Value	179 calories 22.3 g protein 4.3 g lipids
Food Exchanges	2 oz meat 1/2 bread exchange
Cooking Time	4 min
Standing Time	None
Power Level	90%
Write Your Cooking Time Here	

Ingredients
450 g (1 lb) sole fillets
125 mL (1/2 cup) Italian-style breadcrumbs
50 mL (1/4 cup) Parmesan cheese, grated
salt and pepper to taste
125 mL (1/2 cup) milk

Method
— Combine the breadcrumbs, Parmesan cheese, salt and pepper; mix well.
— Soak the fillets in the milk and then bread them with the breadcrumb mixture.
— Arrange the fillets on a rack, placing the fleshy parts toward the outside.
— Cook uncovered at 90% for 2 minutes. Give the dish a half-turn.
— Continue cooking at 90% for 2 minutes or until the fillets are cooked.

To ensure even cooking, give the dish a half-turn halfway through the cooking time.

MICROTIPS

Different Types of Breading

As well as enhancing the flavor of fish, breading can produce infinite variations on the range of recipes already available. Instead of buying breadcrumbs, you can make them yourself with salted crackers, cereals, stale bread, graham crackers and so on. In fact the only limits are your culinary preferences and your own imagination. Of course, you can also add sesame seeds or poppy seeds, herbs and many other ingredients to flavor the breading.

Sole Roulades with a Tropical Sauce

Level of Difficulty	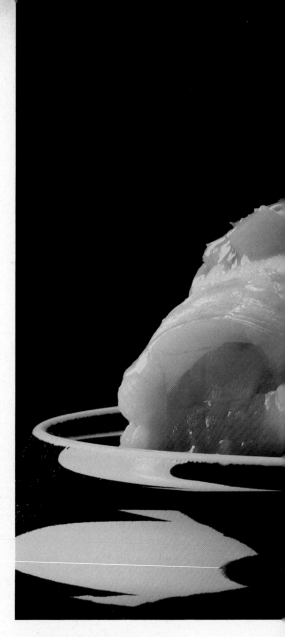
Preparation Time	15 min
Cost per Serving	$
Number of Servings	6
Nutritional Value	193 calories 34.9 g protein 6.63 g lipids
Food Exchanges	2 oz meat 1 vegetable exchange 1/2 fruit exchange
Cooking Time	18 min
Standing Time	4 min
Power Level	100%, 70%
Write Your Cooking Time Here	

Ingredients
900 g (2 lb) sole fillets
250 mL (1 cup) carrots, grated
50 mL (1/4 cup) onions, finely chopped
30 mL (2 tablespoons) butter
1 540 mL (19 oz) can crushed pineapple
125 mL (1/2 cup) green pepper, finely sliced
30 mL (2 tablespoons) vinegar
30 mL (2 tablespoons) brown sugar
30 mL (2 tablespoons) cornstarch
15 mL (1 tablespoon) soy sauce

Method
— Put the carrots, onions and butter in a casserole; cover and cook at 100% for 2 to 3 minutes.
— Drain the pineapple and reserve 250 mL (1 cup) of the juice.
— Add the 250 mL of the crushed pineapple (about half the can) to the carrot and onion mixture. Set the remainder aside.
— Spread the fillets with this mixture. Roll them up and secure with toothpicks.
— Put the rolls into a dish; cover and cook at 70% for 4 minutes.
— Move the fillets from the center of the dish to the outside and vice versa. Continue cooking at 70% for 4 minutes or until the fish can be easily flaked. Let stand for 4 minutes.
— Put the green pepper into a dish; cover and cook at 100% for 1 to 2 minutes. Set aside.
— Combine the reserved pineapple juice, the vinegar, brown sugar, cornstarch and soy sauce

48

in a bowl.
— Cook at 100% for 3 to 4 minutes or until the sauce thickens, stirring every 2 minutes.
— Add the remaining pineapple and the green pepper to the sauce and reheat at 100% for 1 minute or until hot.
— Pour over the roulades and serve.

MICROTIPS

Choosing the Right Sauce

All sauces are not appropriate for all kinds of fish. Fish with delicate textures, such as sole or halibut, are best served with light sauces that will not mask their flavor.

On the other hand, richly flavored fish, such as mackerel, are delicious served with a zippy, lemony sauce. The taste of poached fish is exceptional with an herb sauce.

Pickerel Stuffed with Green Grapes and Almonds

Level of Difficulty	🍴🍴🍴
Preparation Time	10 min
Cost per Serving	$ $
Number of Servings	4
Nutritional Value	345 calories 36.18 g protein 18.5 g lipids
Food Exchanges	4 oz meat 1/4 fruit exchange 1/2 bread exchange 2-1/2 fat exchanges 1/4 milk exchange
Cooking Time	26 min
Standing Time	5 min
Power Level	100%, 70%
Write Your Cooking Time Here	

Ingredients
1 pickerel, 675 g (1-1/2 lb),
cleaned and trimmed
salt and pepper to taste
50 mL (1/4 cup) butter
50 mL (1/4 cup) slivered
almonds
150 mL (2/3 cup) green
seedless grapes, cut into
quarters
250 mL (1 cup) croutons
50 mL (1/4 cup) celery, finely
sliced
15 mL (1 tablespoon) parsley,
chopped
150 mL (2/3 cup) plain
yoghurt
oil to brush the fish

Method
— Sponge the inside and
  outside of the fish with a
  damp cloth; season the
  cavity with salt and
  pepper.
— Melt the butter at 100%
  for 1 minute.
— Add the almonds and cook
  at 100% for 3 to 5
  minutes, stirring once
  during the cooking time.
— Add the grapes, croutons,
  celery, parsley and
  yoghurt. Mix well.
— Stuff the fish with this
  mixture and secure with
  toothpicks.
— Brush the fish with oil and
  cover each end with
  aluminum foil.

⟹

Pickerel Stuffed with Green Grapes and Almonds

After cleaning and trimming the fish, carefully sponge it, inside and out, with a damp cloth.

Melt the butter and cook the almonds.

Stuff the fish with the almond and grape mixture.

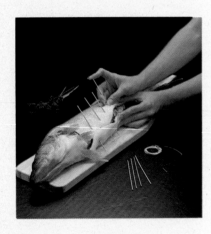

Secure the fish with toothpicks so that it keeps its shape during cooking.

Brush the fish with oil before cooking.

Cover the ends of the fish with aluminum foil to prevent overcooking.

— Put the fish in a baking dish and cook at 70% for 10 minutes.

— Give the dish a half-turn and continue cooking at 70% for another 8 to 10 minutes.

— Let stand for 5 minutes and serve.

Pickerel Fillets Sautéed in Butter

Level of Difficulty	🍴🍴
Preparation Time	10 min
Cost per Serving	$
Number of Servings	4
Nutritional Value	228 calories 21.7 g protein 16.1 g lipids
Food Exchanges	2 oz meat 1-1/2 fat exchanges
Cooking Time	5 min
Standing Time	5 min
Power Level	100%, 90%
Write Your Cooking Time Here	

Ingredients
4 pickerel fillets
50 mL (1/4 cup) butter
15 mL (1 teaspoon) oil
10 mL (2 teaspoons) parsley, chopped

Method
— Heat a browning dish at 100% for 7 minutes.
— Add the butter and the oil; heat at 100% for 30 seconds.
— Sear the fillets on both sides.
— Cover and cook at 90% for 4 to 5 minutes.
— Let stand for 5 minutes and garnish with parsley before serving.

Bouillabaisse

Level of Difficulty	🍴🍴
Preparation Time	40 min
Cost per Serving	$ $
Number of Servings	8
Nutritional Value	185 calories 26.8 g protein 20.05 g lipids
Food Exchanges	2 oz meat 2 vegetable exchanges
Cooking Time	31 min
Standing Time	None
Power Level	100%, 70%
Write Your Cooking Time Here	

Ingredients

900 g (2 lb) whole fish, with their heads
12 mussels in their shells
225 g (8 oz) fresh shrimps
225 g (8 oz) scallops
75 mL (1/3 cup) olive oil
2 onions, sliced
3 leeks, white parts only, chopped
2 cloves garlic, crushed
4 tomatoes, peeled and crushed
250 mL (1 cup) dry white wine
500 mL (2 cups) vegetable bouillon
15 mL (1 tablespoon) salt
10 mL (2 teaspoons) sugar
pinch saffron
1 bay leaf
pinch fennel
15 mL (1 tablespoon) fresh parsley, chopped

Method

— Heat a browning dish at 100% for 7 minutes.
— Add the oil and heat at 100% for 30 seconds.
— Add the onions, leeks and garlic and sear.
— Transfer the seared vegetables to a casserole; add the tomatoes, wine, vegetable bouillon, salt, sugar, saffron, bay leaf, fennel and parsley to the casserole. Cover and bring to a boil. Cook at 100% for 15 minutes.
— In the meantime, clean and trim the fish, cut it into pieces and reserve the heads for fish stock.
— Brush the mussels clean.
— Shell and devein the shrimps; rinse the scallops under running water.
— Add the fish, shrimps and scallops to the soup base.
— Cover and cook at 100% for 10 minutes or until the fish is almost cooked. Set aside.
— In another dish, arrange the mussels in a single layer and cook at 70% for 3 to 4 minutes or until the shells open.
— Add the open mussels to the soup and cook uncovered at 70% for 2 minutes.

Fish and Zucchini Chowder

Level of Difficulty	![fork knife spoon icon]
Preparation Time	20 min
Cost per Serving	$
Number of Servings	4
Nutritional Value	233 calories 22.2 g protein 7.9 g lipids
Food Exchanges	2 oz meat 1-1/2 fat exchanges 1 vegetable exchange 1/2 bread exchange
Cooking Time	28 min
Standing Time	None
Power Level	100%
Write Your Cooking Time Here	

Ingredients
450 g (1 lb) fish fillets
30 mL (2 tablespoons) butter
125 mL (1/2 cup) onions, chopped
250 mL (1 cup) potatoes, cubed
125 mL (1/2 cup) turnips, cubed
250 mL (1 cup) carrots, sliced
500 mL (2 cups) hot chicken bouillon
375 mL (1-1/2 cups) hot milk
50 mL (1/4 cup) pimento, chopped
2 mL (1/2 teaspoon) thyme
2 mL (1/2 teaspoon) celery salt
salt and pepper to taste
375 mL (1-1/2 cups) zucchini, unpeeled and sliced
15 mL (1 tablespoon) parsley, chopped

Method
— Cut the fish fillets into 2.5 cm (1 in) cubes. Set aside.
— In a bowl or casserole melt the butter at 100% for 30 seconds.
— Add the onions, potatoes, turnips and carrots. Cover and cook at 100% for 5 minutes.
— Stir the vegetables and move those from the outside of the casserole toward the center and vice versa.
— Cover and continue cooking at 100% for 3 minutes.
— Add the bouillon, hot milk, pimento, thyme, celery salt, salt and pepper.
— Cover and bring to a boil at 100%. Cook for 8 to 12 minutes.
— Add the fish and the zucchini. Cover and continue cooking at 100% for 5 to 7 minutes or until the fish is cooked.
— Garnish with parsley and serve.

MICROTIPS

Practical Suggestions for Cooking Vegetables

— Choose vegetables of equal size and shape to ensure even cooking.
— Increase the cooking time as you increase the quantity of vegetables to be cooked together.
— During cooking keep the dish covered and use as little liquid as possible.
— Salt the vegetables *after* cooking, not before.

Combine the ingredients required for the preparation of this special dish, one that will surprise and delight your guests.

Fish and Fruit Kebabs

Level of Difficulty	🍴
Preparation Time	25 min*
Cost per Serving	**$**
Number of Servings	4
Nutritional Value	140 calories 17.6 g protein
Food Exchanges	2 oz meat 1/2 fruit exchange
Cooking Time	6 min
Standing Time	None
Power Level	90%
Write Your Cooking Time Here	✏️

Ingredients
450 g (1 lb) fish fillets
8 pineapple chunks
1 apple, cut into 8
1 peach, cut into 8
1 pear, cut into 8

Marinade:
125 mL (1/2 cup) oil
75 mL (1/3 cup) orange juice
30 mL (2 tablespoons) soy sauce
10 mL (2 teaspoons) orange zest, grated
15 mL (1 tablespoon) parsley, chopped
30 mL (2 tablespoons) onion, grated
2 mL (1/2 teaspoon) salt
2 mL (1/2 teaspoon) pepper

* The fish and fruit must be left to marinate for at least 30 minutes at room temperature or for 1 hour in the refrigerator before cooking.

Method
— Combine all the marinade
ingredients and mix well.
— Cut the fish fillets into 16
pieces.
— Add the fish and the pieces
of fruit to the marinade.
— Marinate for 30 minutes at
room temperature or for 1
hour in the refrigerator,
stirring once carefully.
— Prepare the skewers,
adding first the pineapple
and then alternate the fish
with the other fruit,
ending with pineapple.
— Suspend the skewers on
the ends of a microwave-
safe dish. Brush with the
marinade.
— Cook at 90% for 3
minutes.
— Turn the skewers over and
brush with the marinade;
move the skewers from
the center of the dish to
the outside.
— Continue cooking at 90%
for 3 minutes longer.

MICROTIPS

Preparing Butter
Meunière

To make butter
meunière, simply add
clarified butter to the
pan in which the fish was
cooked and heat until
golden. Add some lemon
juice and freshly
chopped parsley and stir
well. Butter meunière
can be served with fish
and other seafoods.

Fish and Fruit Kebabs

Combine all the marinade ingredients and leave the fish and fruit to marinate for at least 30 minutes at room temperature.

Prepare the skewers by beginning with a piece of pineapple, then alternating the pieces of fish with the other fruit.

Halfway through cooking, move the skewers from the center of the dish to the outside and vice versa.

Wines To Serve with Fish

Although there are no fixed rules for serving wine with fish, there is a strong tradition which favors serving white wine with fish and seafood. In this spirit we present some suggestions for white wines to be served with fish. Chablis, Saint-Véran and Pouilly-Fumé will enhance the taste of cod, sole or turbot dishes. The flavor of tuna or sturgeon will be truly extraordinary when served with a mellow white wine, such as Anjou or Meursault. A white Graves or Sancerre should be served with sea pike. Fish prepared *au gratin* is delicious with an Alsatian wine. Fish patés can be served with dry white wines from any region.

And most important, don't forget to chill the wine!

Haddock Poached in Milk

Ingredients
1 haddock steak, 900 g to 1.3 kg (2 to 3 lb)
500 mL (2 cups) milk
125 mL (1/2 cup) water
1 onion, peeled and studded
with 3 cloves
1 carrot, cut into sticks
1 bay leaf
15 mL (1 tablespoon) cold butter

Method
— Wrap the fish steak in cheesecloth and set aside.
— Pour the milk and water into a casserole; add the onion, carrot and bay leaf.
— Cover and bring to the boil at 100% for 10 to 12 minutes.
— Add the fish; cover and cook at 70% for 15 to 17 minutes.
— Check for doneness; continue cooking if necessary.
— Carefully remove the fish from the cheesecloth.
— Rub the fish with butter as a garnish and serve.

Level of Difficulty	🍴
Preparation Time	10 min
Cost per Serving	$
Number of Servings	6
Nutritional Value	259 calories 42.9 g protein 5.8 g lipids
Food Exchanges	3 oz meat 1/4 milk exchange
Cooking Time	29 min
Standing Time	None
Power Level	100%, 70%
Write Your Cooking Time Here	

Norway Haddock with Herb Sauce

Level of Difficulty	🍴
Preparation Time	10 min
Cost per Serving	$
Number of Servings	4
Nutritional Value	199 calories 25.5 g protein 6.1 g lipids
Food Exchanges	2.5 oz meat 1 vegetable exchange 1-1/2 fat exchanges
Cooking Time	13 min
Standing Time	None
Power Level	100%
Write Your Cooking Time Here	

Ingredients

450 g (1 lb) Norway haddock, cut into fillets
750 mL (3 cups) Chinese lettuce, chopped
50 mL (1/4 cup) onion, finely chopped
15 mL (1 tablespoon) parsley, chopped
1 clove garlic, crushed
1 mL (1/4 teaspoon) thyme
pinch tarragon
125 mL (1/2 cup) hot water
75 mL (1/3 cup) dry white wine
1 bay leaf
30 mL (2 tablespoons) butter
30 mL (2 tablespoons) flour
3 mL (3/4 teaspoon) basil
3 mL (3/4 teaspoon) chervil
2 mL (1/2 teaspoon) dill

Method

— Combine the lettuce, onion, parsley, garlic, thyme and tarragon.
— Arrange half this mixture in a dish, spreading it evenly.
— Put the fillets on top, placing them so that the fleshy parts are toward the outside of the dish.
— Add the remaining lettuce mixture, the hot water, the wine and the bay leaf.
— Cover and cook at 100% for 5 to 6 minutes or until the fish is cooked.
— Remove the fillets and the lettuce mixture from the dish; cover and set aside.
— Pour the cooking liquid into a bowl and set aside.
— Melt the butter at 100% for 30 seconds in the dish in which the fish was cooked.
— Add the flour and mix well.
— Pour in the cooking liquid, the basil, chervil and dill.
— Cook at 100% for 4 to 6 minutes, stirring every 2 minutes or until the sauce thickens.
— Pour the sauce over the fillets and lettuce mixture and serve.

MICROTIPS

To Prevent Fish from Cooking in Its Own Juices

If fillets of fish lose a great deal of liquid during the cooking process, simply spread paper towel under them

at the bottom of the dish or place them on a rack to prevent them from sitting in their own juices. A bacon rack can also be used. In this way the fish will cook evenly, according to the time given in the recipe.

Norway Haddock Fillets on a Bed of Spinach

Level of Difficulty	🍴
Preparation Time	10 min
Cost per Serving	$
Number of Servings	4
Nutritional Value	173 calories 31.1 g protein 1.5 g lipids
Food Exchanges	3 oz meat 1 vegetable exchange
Cooking Time	8 min
Standing Time	None
Power Level	90%, 100%
Write Your Cooking Time Here	

Ingredients
450 g (1 lb) Norway haddock fillets
450 g (1 lb) fresh spinach
15 mL (1 tablespoon) onion, finely chopped
140 mL (5/8 cup) natural yoghurt
125 mL (1/2 cup) cucumber, peeled, seeded and cubed
5 mL (1 teaspoon) lemon juice
pinch nutmeg

Method
— Wash and dry the spinach; arrange it on a cooking platter.
— Wash and pat the fish fillets dry. Place them on top of the spinach, putting the fleshy parts toward the outside of the platter.
— Cover and cook at 90% for 2 minutes.
— Give the dish a half-turn; continue to cook at 90% for 2 minutes or until cooked. Set aside.
— Put the onions in a microwave-safe dish; cover and cook at 100% for 30 to 60 seconds.
— Add the yoghurt, cucumber, lemon juice and nutmeg; cover and cook at 100% for 2 to 3 minutes, stirring once.
— Pour the resulting sauce over the fish and spinach and serve.

Assemble the ingredients needed for this delicious, easy-to-prepare recipe.

MICROTIPS

A Practical Suggestion for Freezing

If carefully packaged in a strong airtight and waterproof wrapping, fish can be kept in the freezer for 6 to 9 months.

Do Not Overcook Fish

Fish will darken in color and its flesh will become tough if cooked for too long or at too high a temperature.

To prevent this outcome, place the thicker, fleshier parts of the fish toward the outside of the dish. Set the cooking time to the minimum time suggested in the recipe and check regularly for doneness.

Mackerel with Leeks

Level of Difficulty	 (cutlery icon)
Preparation Time	10 min
Cost per Serving	**$**
Number of Servings	4
Nutritional Value	388 calories 33.3 g protein 26.5 g lipids
Food Exchanges	4 oz meat 1 vegetable exchange 1-1/2 fat exchanges
Cooking Time	14 min
Standing Time	None
Power Level	100%, 90%
Write Your Cooking Time Here	

Ingredients

2 whole mackerel, 450 g (1 lb) each
30 mL (2 tablespoons) butter
3 leeks, white parts only, finely sliced
1 small *bouquet garni*
125 mL (1/2 cup) fish bouillon
salt to taste
pinch nutmeg

Method

— In a dish melt the butter at 100% for 40 to 50 seconds.
— Add the leeks and the bouquet garni; cover and cook at 100% for 2 to 3 minutes or until the leeks are tender.
— Add the fish bouillon, salt and nutmeg.
— Place the mackerel in another microwave-safe dish.
— Pour the leek mixture over the fish.
— Cover and cook at 90% for 5 minutes.
— Give the dish a half-turn; continue cooking at 90% for 5 minutes or until the fish flakes easily.

Mackerel Fillets with Sweet and Sour Sauce

Level of Difficulty	🍴🍴
Preparation Time	10 min
Cost per Serving	$
Number of Servings	6
Nutritional Value	300 calories 22.2 g protein 20 g lipids
Food Exchanges	3 oz meat 1/2 vegetable exchange 1-1/2 fat exchanges
Cooking Time	11 min
Standing Time	None
Power Level	100%
Write Your Cooking Time Here	

Ingredients
900 g (2 lb) mackerel fillets
30 mL (2 tablespoons) butter
15 mL (1 tablespoon) oil
125 mL (1/2 cup) onions, chopped
125 mL (1/2 cup) celery, finely sliced
1 clove garlic, crushed
30 mL (2 tablespoons) flour
30 mL (2 tablespoons) sugar
2 mL (1/2 teaspoon) salt
2 mL (1/2 teaspoon) pepper
175 mL (3/4 cup) water
50 mL (1/4 cup) vinegar
30 mL (2 tablespoons) parsley, chopped
2 mL (1/2 teaspoon) dill

Method
— Preheat a browning dish at 100% for 7 minutes.
— Add the butter and oil and heat at 100% for 30 seconds.
— Sear the mackerel fillets; remove and set aside.
— Heat the dish at 100% for 60 seconds.
— Sear the onions, celery and garlic.
— Cook at 100% for 2 minutes.
— Sprinkle with flour and mix well. Add the sugar, salt, pepper, water and vinegar; mix well.
— Cook covered at 100% for 4 to 6 minutes, stirring every 2 minutes until the sauce has thickened.
— Add the parsley and dill.
— Carefully put the fillets into the sauce and continue to cook at 100% for 2 to 3 minutes or until the fish is done.

Preheat a browning dish, add the butter and oil and sear the fillets. Set aside.

Sprinkle the mixture of cooked vegetables with the flour and add the sugar, salt, pepper, water and vinegar and mix well.

When the sauce has thickened, add the parsley, dill and fillets and complete the final stage of cooking.

Cod Steaks with Vegetables

Level of Difficulty	🍴🍴
Preparation Time	15 min
Cost per Serving	$
Number of Servings	4
Nutritional Value	439 calories 53 g protein 17.8 g lipids
Food Exchanges	4 oz meat 3 vegetable exchanges 1-1/2 fat exchanges
Cooking Time	19 min
Standing Time	2 min
Power Level	100%, 90%
Write Your Cooking Time Here	

Ingredients
900 g (2 lb) cod steaks
125 mL (1/2 cup) hot water
250 mL (1 cup) potatoes, cubed
250 mL (1 cup) turnips, cubed
125 mL (1/2 cup) celery, cubed
175 mL (3/4 cup) onions, coarsely chopped
175 mL (3/4 cup) leeks, white parts only, coarsely chopped
225 g (8 oz) mushrooms, coarsely chopped
45 mL (3 tablespoons) lemon juice
5 mL (1 teaspoon) black pepper
30 mL (2 tablespoons) fresh parsley, chopped
45 mL (3 tablespoons) butter, melted

Method
— Pour the hot water into a casserole. Add the potatoes, turnips and celery.
— Cover and cook at 100% for 6 minutes.
— Add the onions and leeks; continue to cook at 100% for 5 minutes.
— Add the mushrooms, mix well, cover and let stand for 2 minutes.
— Put the cod steaks into another dish and sprinkle with lemon juice. Add the pepper.
— Pour the vegetable mixture over and around the fish. Cover and cook at 90% for 4 minutes.
— Give the dish a half-turn. Continue to cook at 90% for 4 minutes or until the fish is cooked. Remove the steaks and put them on a platter.
— Garnish with the parsley and melted butter. Serve the vegetables on the side.

Put the steaks into a microwave-safe dish, placing the fleshy parts toward the outside.

After cooking the vegetables in two stages, add them to the fish.

MICROTIPS

To Defrost and Cook Fish Sticks

To defrost and cook fish sticks, preheat a browning dish at 100% for 7 minutes. Add 15 mL (1 tablespoon) of oil and brown the fish. Continue to cook at 100% until the center of the fish sticks is opaque and the flesh can be flaked with a fork.

Perch with Tomatoes

Level of Difficulty	
Preparation Time	5 min
Cost per Serving	$
Number of Servings	4
Nutritional Value	426 calories 47.3 g protein 19.6 g lipids
Food Exchanges	4 oz meat 2 fat exchanges 1 vegetable exchange
Cooking Time	12 min
Standing Time	5 min
Power Level	100%, 70%
Write Your Cooking Time Here	

Ingredients
1 perch, 1.3 kg (3 lb)
pepper to taste
2 mL (1/2 teaspoon) oregano
15 mL (1 tablespoon) lemon juice
45 mL (3 tablespoons) olive oil
4 ripe tomatoes, peeled and sliced
30 mL (2 tablespoons) fresh parsley, chopped
3 onions, sliced
lemon slices to garnish

Method
— Wash and pat the fish dry.
— Combine the pepper, oregano and lemon juice.
— Brush the inside and outside of the perch with the lemon juice mixture. Set aside.
— Combine the oil, tomatoes and parsley. Set aside.
— Cover and cook the onions at 100% for 2 to 3 minutes and combine with the tomato mixture. Put half this mixture in a casserole.
— Place the fish on top of this mixture and cover with the remaining onion and tomato mixture; cook covered at 70% for 9 minutes.
— Give the dish a half-turn and continue to cook, covered, at 70% for 7 to 9 minutes or until the flesh is tender.
— Let stand for 5 minutes.
— Garnish with lemon slices and serve.

Brush the inside and outside of the fish with the mixture of pepper, oregano and lemon juice.

Place the fish in a casserole on top of half the prepared onion and tomato mixture and cover the fish with the remainder of the mixture.

To ensure even cooking, give the dish a half-turn halfway through the cooking time.

Tuna Omelette

Level of Difficulty	
Preparation Time	10 min
Cost per Serving	$
Number of Servings	4
Nutritional Value	407 calories 43.7 g protein 23.3 g lipids
Food Exchanges	5 oz meat 1/2 vegetable exchange 1-1/2 fat exchanges
Cooking Time	9 min
Standing Time	None
Power Level	100%, 70%, 50%
Write Your Cooking Time Here	

Ingredients
1 426 mL (15 oz) can tuna
30 mL (2 tablespoons) butter
1 onion, finely chopped
pepper to taste
5 eggs
15 mL (1 tablespoon) flour
15 mL (1 tablespoon) parsley, chopped

Method
— In a pie plate, melt the butter at 100% for 40 seconds.
— Add the onion and cook at 100% for 2 minutes.
— Flake the tuna and add it to the cooked onion; season with pepper. Set aside.
— Combine the eggs with the flour and beat vigorously.
— Add to the tuna and onion mixture. Mix well and add the parsley.
— Place on a raised rack and cook at 70% for 2 minutes. Lift up the edges of the omelette to distribute the uncooked egg evenly.
— Continue cooking at 50% for 4 minutes or until the omelette is cooked, giving the dish a half-turn halfway through the cooking time.

Tuna Steaks
with Hollandaise Sauce

Level of Difficulty	🍴
Preparation Time	5 min
Cost per Serving	$ $
Number of Servings	4
Nutritional Value	524 calories 43 g protein 34.3 g lipids
Food Exchanges	5 oz meat 3 fat exchanges 1/4 milk exchange
Cooking Time	11 min
Standing Time	2 min
Power Level	100%, 70%
Write Your Cooking Time Here	

Ingredients
4 tuna steaks
60 mL (4 tablespoons) butter
30 mL (2 tablespoons) flour
2 mL (1/2 teaspoon) salt
1 mL (1/4 teaspoon) white pepper
250 mL (1 cup) milk
2 egg yolks, beaten
30 mL (2 tablespoons) lemon juice
zest of half a lemon
salt and pepper to taste
15 mL (1 tablespoon) oil

Method
— To make the sauce, melt 30 mL (2 tablespoons) of the butter; add the flour, salt, white pepper and milk; cook at 100% for 2 minutes.
— Whisk and continue to cook at 100% for 1 minute or until creamy.
— Add the egg yolks and whisk to mix well. Add the lemon juice and zest. Cook at 100% for 1 minute. Whisk and continue cooking at 100% for 30 seconds.
— Add the remaining butter. Stir and season. Cover and set the sauce aside.
— Heat a browning dish at 100% for 7 minutes.
— Add the oil and heat at 100% for 30 seconds; sear the steaks.
— Cook the steaks at 70% for 4 to 6 minutes or until they are done.
— Let stand for 2 minutes and garnish with the sauce before serving.

Add the flour, salt, pepper and milk to the melted butter; whisk and cook until the mixture is creamy.

Add the beaten egg yolks, whisking well, and add the lemon juice and zest; whisk again, cook and add the remaining butter. Season and set aside.

Preheat a browning dish; add the oil and sear the steaks.

Tuna Tetrazzini

Level of Difficulty	🍴
Preparation Time	20 min
Cost per Serving	$
Number of Servings	4
Nutritional Value	475 calories 44.1 g protein 19.9 g lipids
Food Exchanges	4 oz meat 3/4 milk exchange 1 bread exchange 1-1/2 fat exchanges
Cooking Time	21 min
Standing Time	None
Power Level	100%, 70%
Write Your Cooking Time Here	

Ingredients
1 426 mL (15 oz) can tuna
30 mL (2 tablespoons) butter
50 mL (1/4 cup) onions, chopped
125 mL (1/2 cup) canned mushrooms with their liquid
75 mL (1/3 cup) green pepper, finely chopped
30 mL (2 tablespoons) flour
2 mL (1/2 teaspoon) salt
2 mL (1/2 teaspoon) pepper
1 mL (1/4 teaspoon) nutmeg
milk, enough to add to the mushroom liquid to obtain 675 mL (2-3/4 cups)
75 mL (1/3 cup) Parmesan cheese
225 g (8 oz) cooked spaghettini
15 mL (1 tablespoon) red pepper, cooked and chopped

Method
— Melt the butter at 100% for 40 seconds.
— Add the onions, mushrooms (drained) and green pepper. Cover and cook at 100% for 3 to 4 minutes.
— Add the flour and the seasonings; mix well. Cook at 100% for 30 to 40 seconds.
— Blend in the mixture of milk and mushroom liquid and stir until smooth. Cook at 100% for 4 to 6 minutes or until the sauce thickens, stirring every 2 minutes.
— Sprinkle 50 mL (1/4 cup) of the Parmesan cheese over the cooked spaghettini; mix well and put in a dish.
— Crumble the tuna over the spaghettini.
— Add the red pepper to the sauce and pour over the tuna.
— Sprinkle with the remaining Parmesan.
— Cook uncovered at 70% for 7 to 9 minutes, giving the dish a half-turn after 4 minutes.

Cook the vegetables in the butter; add the flour and the seasonings, and mix well.

Add 50 mL (1/4 cup) of the Parmesan cheese to the cooked spaghettini and mix well.

Pour the creamy sauce over the spaghettini and flaked tuna.

Tuna au Gratin

Level of Difficulty	
Preparation Time	20 min
Cost per Serving	$
Number of Servings	4
Nutritional Value	338 calories 25 g protein 17.3 g lipids
Food Exchanges	3 oz meat 1 bread exchange 1/4 milk exchange 2 fat exchanges
Cooking Time	12 min
Standing Time	None
Power Level	100%, 70%
Write Your Cooking Time Here	

Ingredients
1 213 mL (7-1/2 oz) can tuna
45 mL (3 tablespoons) butter
50 mL (1/4 cup) onion, finely chopped
30 mL (2 tablespoons) flour
salt and pepper to taste
15 mL (1 tablespoon) parsley, chopped
375 mL (1-1/2 cups) milk
15 mL (1 tablespoon) red pepper, cooked and diced
375 mL (1-1/2 cups) mashed potatoes
375 mL (1-1/2 cups) grated mozzarella cheese
paprika to garnish

Method
— Melt the butter at 100% for 50 seconds.
— Add the onion and cook at 100% for 2 minutes.
— Add the flour, salt, pepper, parsley and mix well.
— Blend in the milk. Cook at 100% for 4 to 5 minutes or until the sauce thickens, stirring every 2 minutes.
— Add the tuna and the cooked red pepper to the sauce and stir gently.
— Pour in a casserole.

— Arrange the mashed potatoes on top of the mixture around the outside edge of the dish. Add the grated mozzarella to the center of the dish.
— Sprinkle with paprika.
— Cook at 70% for 3 to 4 minutes or until the cheese is melted, giving the dish a half-turn halfway through the cooking time.

Add the tuna and the cooked red pepper to the sauce and stir gently.

Arrange the mashed potatoes on the mixture around the edge of the dish. Use a spoon or a pastry bag.

Sprinkle with paprika before the final stage of cooking.

Smelts in a Rosy Sauce

Ingredients
450 g (1 lb) cleaned smelts
50 mL (1/4 cup) melted butter
15 mL (1 tablespoon) lemon juice

125 mL (1/2 cup) breadcrumbs
50 mL (1/4 cup) olive oil
Sauce:
125 mL (1/2 cup) mayonnaise

2 green onions, finely chopped
chervil and tarragon to taste
30 mL (2 tablespoons) tomato paste
30 mL (2 tablespoons) chili sauce
15 mL (1 tablespoon) horseradish
50 mL (1/4 cup) cucumber, peeled, seeded and diced
50 mL (1/4 cup) watercress, finely chopped

Level of Difficulty	🍴🔪
Preparation Time	15 min
Cost per Serving	$
Number of Servings	4
Nutritional Value	375 calories 10.8 g protein 34.7 g lipids
Food Exchanges	2 oz meat 4 fat exchanges
Cooking Time	4 min
Standing Time	None
Power Level	100%, 90%
Write Your Cooking Time Here	

Method
— Dry the smelts well and brush them with the melted butter combined with the lemon juice.
— Coat the smelts with the breadcrumbs.
— Preheat a browning dish at 100% for 7 minutes.
— Add the oil and heat at 100% for 30 seconds.
— Sear the smelts on both sides.
— Cook uncovered at 90% for 3 to 4 minutes.
— Combine all the ingredients for the sauce, mix well and serve at room temperature with the smelts.

Burbot with Lemon Butter

Ingredients
450 g (1 lb) burbot
30 mL (2 tablespoons) butter
15 mL (1 tablespoon) oil
pepper to taste

50 mL (1/4 cup) butter
30 mL (2 tablespoons) lemon juice
30 mL (2 tablespoons) fresh parsley, chopped

Method
— Preheat a browning dish at 100% for 7 minutes.
— Add the 30 mL (2 tablespoons) butter and the oil and heat at 100% for 30 seconds.
— Sear the burbot; season with pepper.
— Cook at 90% for 3 to 4 minutes or until the fish is cooked.
— Cover and set aside.
— Melt the 50 mL (1/4 cup) butter at 100% for 90 seconds.
— Add the lemon juice and parsley, and mix well.
— Pour the lemon butter over the burbot and serve.

Level of Difficulty	🍴
Preparation Time	10 min
Cost per Serving	$
Number of Servings	4
Nutritional Value	371 calories 14 g protein 32 g lipids
Food Exchanges	3 oz meat 3 fat exchanges
Cooking Time	6 min
Standing Time	None
Power Level	100%, 90%
Write Your Cooking Time Here	✏️

Yellow Perch with Beer

Level of Difficulty	 🍴
Preparation Time	15 min
Cost per Serving	$
Number of Servings	6
Nutritional Value	286 calories 34.2 g protein 12.3 g lipids
Food Exchanges	4 oz meat 1 vegetable exchange 1 fat exchange
Cooking Time	8 min
Standing Time	None
Power Level	100%, 90%
Write Your Cooking Time Here	

Ingredients

900 g (2 lb) yellow perch fillets
15 mL (1 tablespoon) oil
30 mL (2 tablespoons) butter
2 celery stalks, finely sliced
3 onions, finely sliced
30 mL (2 tablespoons) flour
125 mL (1/2 cup) beer
30 mL (2 tablespoons) Dijon
mustard

Method

— Preheat a browning dish at
  100% for 7 minutes.
— Add the oil and butter.
  Heat at 100% for 30
  seconds.
— Sear the fillets and remove
  them; set aside.
— Heat the browning dish at
  100% for 1 minute and
  sear the vegetables.
— Add the flour and mix
  well.
— Blend in the beer and
  mustard; mix well.
— Put the fillets into the
  sauce. Cover and cook at
  90% for 8 minutes.

Halibut Fillets with Broccoli

Level of Difficulty	🍴
Preparation Time	15 min
Cost per Serving	$
Number of Servings	4
Nutritional Value	246 calories 28 g protein 13.5 g lipids
Food Exchanges	3 oz meat 1 vegetable exchange
Cooking Time	7 min
Standing Time	None
Power Level	70%
Write Your Cooking Time Here	

Ingredients
450 g (1 lb) halibut fillets
225 g (8 oz) broccoli, stalks with flowerets
30 mL (2 tablespoons) water
2 mL (1/2 teaspoon) tarragon
2 mL (1/2 teaspoon) parsley, chopped
2 mL (1/2 teaspoon) chives
salt and pepper to taste
15 mL (1 tablespoon) butter
125 mL (1/2 cup) cheddar cheese, grated

Method
— Place 1 or 2 stalks of broccoli on each fillet, with the flowerets toward the outer edges. Carefully roll up each fillet and secure with toothpicks.
— Place in a baking dish, add the water and all the seasoning; garnish with butter.
— Cover and cook at 70% for 3 to 5 minutes or until the fish becomes opaque, rearranging the fillets so that those in the center of the dish are toward the outside and vice versa after 3 minutes of cooking time.
— Garnish with the grated cheese.
— Cook at 70% for 1 to 2 minutes or until the cheese is melted.

Place 1 or 2 stalks of broccoli on each fillet, with the flowerets at the outer edges. Roll up and secure with toothpicks.

After the first stage of cooking, move the fillets from the center of the dish to the outside and vice versa.

Garnish with grated cheddar cheese before the final stage of cooking.

MICROTIPS

How To Choose Broccoli

Make sure that the head of broccoli is firm and compact and the color is a good dark green, almost mauve in spots. The stalks should be firm but not woody and a paler green in color. Reject broccoli showing small yellow flowerets in the bouquet or broccoli with damp surfaces.

Halibut Steaks in Lettuce Leaves

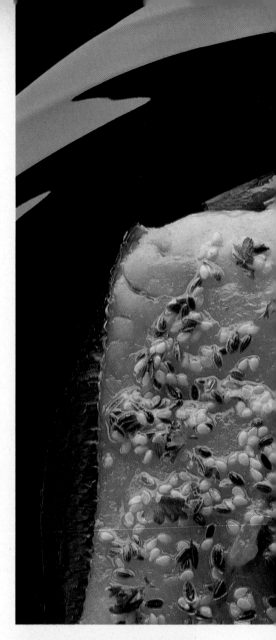

Level of Difficulty	🍴
Preparation Time	10 min
Cost per Serving	**$**
Number of Servings	4
Nutritional Value	395 calories 35.5 g protein 23 g lipids
Food Exchanges	4 oz meat 2 vegetable exchanges 2-1/2 fat exchanges
Cooking Time	14 min
Standing Time	4 min
Power Level	90%, 70%
Write Your Cooking Time Here	

Ingredients
4 halibut steaks
1 head Boston lettuce
1 onion, diced
15 mL (1 tablespoon) parsley, chopped
1 bay leaf
50 mL (1/4 cup) oil
125 mL (1/2 cup) dry white wine
1 chicken bouillon cube, crushed

Method
— Arrange some of the lettuce leaves in the bottom of a shallow baking dish. Sprinkle the onion and parsley on the lettuce; add the bay leaf and the halibut steaks.
— Combine the oil and white wine, and mix well. Pour over the fish.
— Sprinkle the crushed chicken bouillon cube over the fish. Cover with the remaining lettuce leaves. Cook at 90% for 6 minutes.
— Give the dish a half-turn. Continue cooking at 70% for 7 to 8 minutes or until the fish is cooked.
— Let stand for 4 minutes and remove the steaks. Serve with the lettuce and a sauce of your choice.

Assemble all the ingredients required for this recipe, which combines flavorful gifts of the sea with the goodness of the earth.

Arrange some of the lettuce leaves in the bottom of a shallow baking dish.

Sprinkle the onion and parsley over the lettuce; add the bay leaf and the halibut steaks.

MICROTIPS

To Defrost Fish Steaks

Defrost fish steaks at 30% for 9 to 15 minutes per kilogram (4 to 7 min/lb), separating the steaks and giving the dish a half-turn halfway through the defrosting time. Allow a standing time equal to one quarter of the total defrosting time. Check the fish. If necessary, continue defrosting until it can be flaked.

Red Mullet *en Papillote*

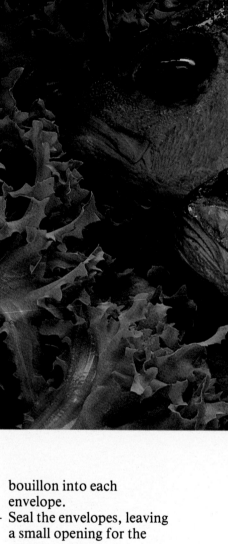

Level of Difficulty	
Preparation Time	15 min
Cost per Serving	$
Number of Servings	4
Nutritional Value	327 calories 43.8 g protein 12.29 g lipids
Food Exchanges	4 oz meat 1 vegetable exchange 1 fat exchange
Cooking Time	10 min
Standing Time	5 min
Power Level	70%
Write Your Cooking Time Here	

Ingredients

2 red mullets, 450 g (1 lb) each
salt and pepper to taste
30 mL (2 tablespoons) olive oil
2 carrots, finely sliced
2 onions, finely chopped
2 green onions, finely chopped
10 mL (2 teaspoons) chervil
10 mL (2 teaspoons) fine herbs
1 bay leaf
50 mL (1/4 cup) chicken bouilllon

Method

— Clean, rinse and dry the mullets; salt and pepper the cavities.
— Prepare two envelopes for the fish; lay each fish on a piece of plastic wrap placed over a piece of waxed paper. Brush the fish with the olive oil.
— Spread the vegetables and seasonings evenly over the fish.
— Close the envelopes, leaving a small opening; put them in a baking dish.
— Pour half the chicken bouillon into each envelope.
— Seal the envelopes, leaving a small opening for the steam to escape.
— Cook at 70% for 9 to 10 minutes or until the fish is cooked; give the dish a half-turn halfway through the cooking time.
— Let stand for 5 minutes before serving.

Arrange the fish on a layer of plastic wrap over a layer of waxed paper; brush with oil and add the vegetables and seasonings.

Put the fish in a baking dish; pour half the chicken bouillon into each envelope and seal, leaving just a small opening for the steam to escape.

Give the dish a half-turn halfway through the cooking time.

Fish Croquettes
with Shrimp Sauce

Level of Difficulty	¶¶¶
Preparation Time	20 min
Cost per Serving	$
Number of Servings	6
Nutritional Value	309 calories 22.2 g protein 11.4 g lipids
Food Exchanges	3 oz meat 1/2 bread exchange 1 fat exchange
Cooking Time	6 min
Standing Time	None
Power Level	100%, 90%
Write Your Cooking Time Here	

Ingredients
450 g (1 lb) cooked fish, flaked
250 mL (1 cup) croutons
50 mL (1/4 cup) milk
1 egg, beaten
30 mL (2 tablespoons) onion, grated
2 mL (1/2 teaspoon) salt
250 mL (1 cup) fine breadcrumbs
30 mL (2 tablespoons) butter
15 mL (1 tablespoon) oil
1 284 mL (10 oz) can cream of shrimp soup, undiluted
125 mL (1/2 cup) milk
10 mL (2 teaspoons) vinegar

Method
— Soak the croutons in the 50 mL (1/4 cup) milk.
— Combine the croutons, fish, beaten egg, onion and salt; mix well.
— Add 50 to 125 mL (1/4 to 1/2 cup) of the breadcrumbs to obtain a firm consistency.
— Form croquettes 5 cm (2 in) round and 2.5 cm (1 in) thick; roll them in the remaining breadcrumbs.
— Preheat a browning dish at 100% for 7 minutes. Add the butter and oil and heat at 100% for 30 seconds.
— Sear the croquettes on both sides.
— Cook uncovered at 90% for 3 minutes or until cooked. Set aside.
— Combine the cream of shrimp soup, 125 mL (1/2 cup) milk and the vinegar. Heat at 100% for 3 minutes.
— Pour the sauce over the croquettes and serve.

Combine the milk-soaked croutons, the fish, beaten egg, onion, salt and some of the breadcrumbs. Shape into croquettes.

Coat the croquettes with the remaining breadcrumbs.

Sear the croquettes on both sides in a preheated browning dish containing the heated butter and oil.

Marinated Salt Herring

Level of Difficulty	
Preparation Time	10 min*
Cost per Serving	$
Number of Servings	2
Nutritional Value	112 calories 5.8 g protein 3.5 g lipids
Food Exchanges	1 oz meat 1 vegetable exchange
Cooking Time	5 min
Standing Time	None
Power Level	100%
Write Your Cooking Time Here	

* Herring fillets must soak for 24 hours in cold water before the marinade is added; they must then be left to marinate for several hours in the refrigerator before serving.

Ingredients
2 salt herrings, skinless and cut into fillets
2 onions, sliced
125 mL (1/2 cup) vinegar
150 mL (2/3 cup) water
250 mL (1 cup) sugar
10 grains allspice, crushed

Method
— Immerse the fillets in cold water and leave to soak for 24 hours.
— Drain and rinse; cut into 1.5 cm (1/2 in) strips.
— Put the strips of herring into a dish. Set aside.
— Combine the onions, vinegar, water, sugar and allspice.
— Cover and cook at 100% for 4 to 5 minutes or until boiling.
— Let cool and pour over the herring.
— Leave to marinate for several hours in the refrigerator before serving.

These ingredients combine to give this recipe for marinated herring a distinctive flavor— one that is saucy and piquant.

MICROTIPS

Restoring Freshness to Food

The microwave oven is a marvellous tool for restoring freshness to food. Stale crackers will regain their crispy texture if heated in the oven at 100% for 10 to 15 seconds and left to stand for a few minutes outside the oven.

To soften brown sugar that has gone hard, just put the sugar into a microwave-safe glass, add a slice of apple and cover with plastic wrap. Heat at 100% for 15 seconds or until the brown sugar has regained its original consistency.

Sea Pike in Caper Sauce

Level of Difficulty	
Preparation Time	10 min
Cost per Serving	$ $
Number of Servings	4
Nutritional Value	301 calories 33.5 g protein 16.5 g lipids
Food Exchanges	3.5 oz meat 3 fat exchanges
Cooking Time	19 min
Standing Time	None
Power Level	100%, 70%
Write Your Cooking Time Here	

Ingredients
1 900 g (2 lb) sea pike
2 mL (1/2 teaspoon) salt
2 mL (1/2 teaspoon) pepper
50 mL (1/4 cup) butter
15 mL (1 tablespoon) oil
45 mL (3 tablespoons) flour
500 mL (2 cups) fish bouillon
10 mL (2 teaspoons) capers
2 anchovy fillets, chopped
2 mL (1/2 teaspoon) sugar
30 mL (2 tablespoons) lemon juice

Method
— Clean and wash the sea pike; salt and pepper the cavity.
— Preheat a browning dish at 100% for 7 minutes.
— Add the butter and oil; heat at 100% for 30 seconds.
— Sear the sea pike. Cover and cook at 70% for 10 minutes or until the fish is cooked. Give the dish a half-turn halfway through the cooking time.
— Remove the fish from the dish and set aside.
— Add the flour to the dish and mix well. Blend in the fish bouillon and whisk.
— Cook at 100% for 5 to 6 minutes or until the sauce thickens, stirring every 2 minutes.
— Add the capers, anchovies, sugar and lemon juice.
— Pour the sauce over the fish. Reheat at 70% for 2 to 3 minutes.

The ingredients for this recipe, which will quickly become an everyday favorite, can be found at the supermarket.

MICROTIPS

To Defrost Haddock Fillets

With the microwave oven in today's kitchen defrosting can be done in minutes. For example, to defrost block-frozen haddock fillets remove their wrapping, place them on a microwave-safe rack and set the power level at 30%.

Defrost for 13 to 22 min/kg (6 to 10 min/lb), separating the fillets and giving the dish a half-turn halfway through the defrosting time. Continue defrosting until the fish is defrosted on the surface and is very cold in the center. Let stand for 10 minutes or until the defrosting is complete.

Entertaining

Menu:
Cream of Asparagus Soup
Mussels Marinière
Salmon Trout with Red Wine
Poached Pears with Raspberry Coulis

There is nothing nicer than sharing a well-planned meal with friends or family, one consisting of dishes in which all the flavors complement each other. The menu we offer for entertaining serves four people and features salmon trout, a choice dish much appreciated by lovers of fine food.

Salmon trout is sure to please the finest palates. Sharing the menu with mussels marinière, a real treat for seafood lovers, the salmon trout with red wine will be an unforgettable experience.

A first course of cream of asparagus soup will stimulate appetites and provide significant nutritional value. The lovely taste of asparagus is ideally suited to a creamy soup.

Finally, a dessert of poached pears with a raspberry coulis —an elegant dessert that will finish your meal on a light note.

From the Recipe to Your Table

Planning a meal for a number of friends or family is hard work and takes a certain amount of organization. Cooking a complete meal in the microwave oven must be planned ahead in the same way as a meal cooked in a conventional oven. Only the cooking and reheating times vary.

24 hours before the meal:
— Poach the pears.
— Prepare the raspberry coulis and refrigerate it.
8 hours before the meal:
— Prepare the cream of asparagus soup and store it at room temperature.
1 hour and 30 minutes before the meal:
— Cook the trout and let stand on a serving platter at room temperature.
1 hour before the meal:
— Arrange the pears and the coulis on a serving platter.
30 minutes before the meal:
— Prepare the mussels and arrange them on a serving platter.
15 minutes before the meal:
— Reheat the cream of asparagus soup at 70% for 10 minutes, stirring once.
5 minutes before the meal:
— Cover the mussels in plastic wrap and reheat at 70% for 5 minutes, giving the dish a half-turn after 2-1/2 minutes.

Cream of Asparagus Soup

Ingredients
1 can asparagus
90 mL (6 tablespoons) butter
1 small onion, finely sliced
90 mL (6 tablespoons) flour
1.5 L (6 cups) hot chicken
bouilllon
1 *bouquet garni,* made with
the following ingredients
wrapped in cheesecloth:
   1 mL (1/4 teaspoon) thyme
   1 bay leaf
   2 mL (1/2 teaspoon) chervil
   1 mL (1/4 teaspoon) basil
   1 clove garlic
   fresh parsley
   celery, chopped
salt and pepper to taste
30 mL (2 tablespoons) 35%
cream
45 mL (3 tablespoons)
asparagus tips for garnish
15 mL (1 tablespoon) parsley,
finely chopped

Method
— In a casserole melt 75 mL
(5 tablespoons) of the
butter at 100% for 50
seconds. Add the onion,
cover and cook at 100%
for 2 minutes. Add the
asparagus, cover and
cook at 100% for 5
minutes; give the dish a
half-turn halfway through
the cooking time.
— Add the flour, mix well
and blend in the chicken
bouillon. Cook uncovered
at 100% for 6 to 7 minutes
or until the mixture
thickens, stirring every 2
minutes.
— Transfer the mixture to a
blender and purée. Return
to the casserole.
— Add the *bouquet garni,*
salt, pepper and cream,
and bring to a boil.
Simmer at 50% for 15
minutes. Remove the
bouquet garni.
— Add the remaining butter,
pour the soup into 4
individual bowls and
garnish with the
asparagus tips and
parsley.

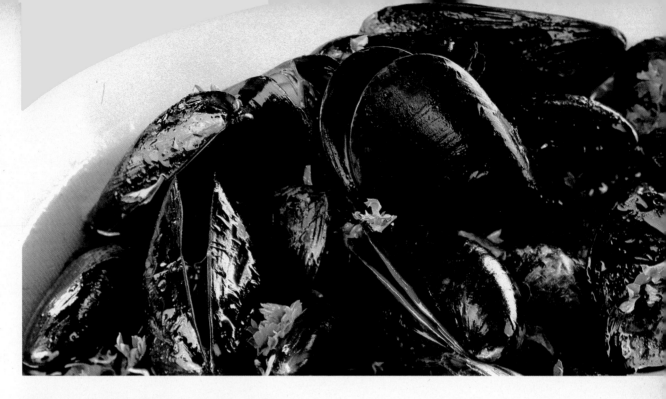

Mussels Marinière

Ingredients
24 mussels, cleaned and scrubbed
75 mL (1/3 cup) butter
2 green onions, finely chopped
1 onion, grated
30 mL (2 tablespoons) fresh parsley, chopped
300 mL (10 oz) dry white wine
pepper to taste

Method
— Melt the butter at 100% for 1 minute.
— Add the green onions, grated onion and parsley.
— Cook at 100% for 3 minutes.
— Add the wine and the pepper. Cook at 100% for 2 minutes.
— Add the mussels. Cover and cook at 100% for 2 to 3 minutes.
— Discard any mussels that do not open.
— Check the seasoning and adjust if necessary.
— Immediately before serving, place the mussels in their shells on a platter and pour the liquid over them.

Salmon Trout with Red Wine

Level of Difficulty	🍴🍴
Preparation Time	20 min
Cost per Serving	$ $ $
Number of Servings	4
Nutritional Value	491 calories 32.5 g protein 33.8 g lipids
Food Exchanges	5 oz meat 4 fat exchanges
Cooking Time	55 min
Standing Time	None
Power Level	100%, 90%, 50%
Write Your Cooking Time Here	

Ingredients
4 whole salmon trout
45 mL (3 tablespoons) butter
45 mL (3 tablespoons) flour
salt and pepper to taste
2 anchovy fillets, ground into
a paste

Stock:
45 mL (3 tablespoons) butter
1 onion, finely sliced
1 small carrot, finely sliced
1 L (4 cups) red wine
500 mL (2 cups) water
bouquet garni
salt and pepper to taste

Method
— First prepare the stock. Melt the butter at 100% for 40 seconds.
— Add the onion and carrot; cover and cook at 100% for 5 minutes, stirring halfway through the cooking time.
— Add the red wine, water, *bouquet garni,* salt and pepper; cover and cook at 100% for 20 minutes. Strain through a fine sieve.
— Put the trout in a dish and pour the stock over the fish. Cover and cook at 90% for 5 minutes.
— Move the trout from the center of the dish to the outside and vice versa. Continue cooking at 90% for 5 minutes or until the trout are cooked.
— Remove the trout and set them aside.
— To make the sauce, strain the stock through a sieve once more. Cook uncovered at 100% for 10 minutes to reduce.
— Combine the butter and flour; knead to make a *beurre manié.* Add, a drop at a time, to the cooking liquid, whisking well.
— Cook at 100% for 4 to 5 minutes or until the sauce thickens, stirring every minute.
— Season with salt and pepper and add the anchovy paste.
— Reheat the trout at 50% for 3 to 4 minutes. Pour the sauce over the fish before serving.

A Choice of Vegetables

Every well-balanced meal needs vegetables. Each season offers a variety from which to choose. In this case, glazed carrots or green beans could be served with the salmon trout. To prepare the carrots, simply peel 225 grams (8 oz) and slice them into equal-sized rounds. Put into a 0.5 L (2 cup) microwave-safe casserole. Add 15 mL (1 tablespoon) of water. Cover and cook at 100% for 6 to 8 minutes, stirring 2 or 3 times during the cooking.

To prepare the green beans, cut 225 grams (8 oz) into 2.5 cm (1 in) pieces and put them into a 0.5 L (2 cup) casserole with 125 mL (1/2 cup) water. Cover and cook at 100% for 7 to 9 minutes, stirring 2 or 3 times.

Poached Pears with Raspberry Coulis

Ingredients
8 pears, peeled but with their stems intact
750 mL (3 cups) water
juice of 1 lemon
375 mL (1-1/2 cups) sugar
zest of 1 lemon
1 450 g (1 lb) box frozen raspberries, defrosted
30 mL (2 tablespoons) pear liqueur
45 mL (3 tablespoons) lemon juice

Method
— In a casserole, combine the water, juice of 1 lemon, 250 mL (1 cup) of the sugar and the lemon zest. Bring to a boil and cook at 100% for 7 to 9 minutes. Stir halfway through the cooking time.
— Carefully plunge the pears into the syrup. Cook at 100% for 3 to 4 minutes, or until the pears are poached but still quite firm. Remove the pears from the syrup and refrigerate.
— Pour the defrosted raspberries into a blender. Add the remaining 125 mL (1 cup) sugar, the liqueur and the lemon juice. Blend until smooth. Strain through a very fine sieve and refrigerate.
— Pour the coulis onto a platter and arrange the pears on top before serving.

MICROTIPS

Cooking Long Grain Rice in the Microwave Oven

Cooking long grain rice in the microwave oven gives spectacular results. With the microwave method, the flavor of the rice is more pronounced and the texture, even fluffier. To prepare the rice, proceed as follows:
— Into a 2 L (8 cup) casserole, pour 500 mL (2 cups) of boiling water, 250 mL (1 cup) of long grain rice and 5 mL (1 teaspoon) salt.
— Cover, leaving a small opening for the steam to escape.
— Cook at 100% for 5 minutes and stir; cover again and continue cooking at 70% for 10 minutes. Let stand for 4 minutes before serving.

Fish Terminology

Like all great arts, the art of cooking has developed a specialized vocabulary over the course of its long history. The terms used may designate methods of preparation or the dishes themselves. Because you will find these terms in the recipes listed in this volume as well as in other cookbooks, we have made a list of some of the more common ones used.

Boning fish: Removing the bones from fish.

Cooking *au bleu*: A method of cooking certain freshwater fish, mainly trout. Consists of plunging the fish, absolutely fresh, if not alive, into a boiling court bouillon. The skin of the fish takes on a bluish hue in reaction to a combination of the slime on the skin and the vinegar in the court bouillon.

Court bouillon: An aromatic lqiuid with the addition of wine, lemon juice or vinegar in which fish and crustaceans are cooked. The court bouillon can be kept from one recipe to another or can be used as the base for a soup or white fish sauce.

Dariole: A small cylindrical mold used in making mousseline, a light smooth-textured preparation based on forcemeat, egg whites and cream. Fish forcemeat is frequently used.

***Dégorger*:** This term refers to soaking a food (snails, for example) in cold water to cleanse it of impurities.

Dressing: The action of preparing a fish for cooking. Dressing includes, among other steps, washing, scaling, trimming and eviscerating.

Eviscerate: The act of removing the entrails (internal organs, gills, coagulated blood, etc.) of a fish.

Fish stock (fumet): A court bouillon to which fish trimmings (heads, bones) are added. Stocks can also be made from shellfish and other seafood. Used to prepare sauces for fish and shellfish.

Paupiette: A fillet of flattened fish, stuffed and rolled.

Poaching: A method of cooking fish that consists of immersing it in liquid and cooking over a very low heat; the liquid must remain below the boiling point.

Quenelle: A type of dumpling made with fish or meat forcemeat, bound with eggs and poached.

Risotto: A method of cooking rice in which it is sautéed in fat before liquid is added.

Roux: A mixture of equal quantities of flour and butter which is cooked and used to thicken sauces.

Salted roe: Fish eggs.

Saltwater: Sea water or freshwater with salt, used to cook fish. It is suggested that saltwater be used only for freshly caught fish.

Scaling: The act of removing the scales of a fish by scraping them off, working from the tail to the head against the ''nap.''

Skinning: The act of removing the skin of fish.

Soft roe: The milt or sperm of male fish, prepared and consumed with the fish or separately as a garnish.

Steak (darne): A thick cross-slice of a large fish.

Tourte: A pastry round filled with meat or fish.

Trimming: The action of cutting off the fins and wattle of a fish.

Turban: A term used to describe a circle-shaped preparation made of fish forcemeat cooked in a border mold.

Zéphir: A light and frothy preparation. Frequently used to describe mousses and mousselines of fish cooked in ramekins and served as appetizers.

Culinary Terms

Have you ever been given a menu and found that you were unable to understand many of the words? Not only are there a number of culinary terms that are obscure but there are many ways to cook pasta or rice that have special terms to describe them. Here is a short glossary of terms with descriptions of their meanings that may help you.

Bouillabaisse: An extremely flavorful fish soup based on combining a variety of fish and shellfish, with saffron, garlic and tomatoes as essential ingredients.

Clam chowder: A chowder based on clams, this dish is typical of the United States. Manhattan clam chowder is based on a tomato liquid whereas New England clam chowder is based on milk.

En colère: A method of presenting fish in which the fish is arranged in a ring (the tail is placed in the mouth). Used mainly for serving whiting.

En papillote: This term is used to describe any preparation that is enclosed in a sheet of paper, sealed and cooked. The food steams and retains all its flavor.

Hollandaise: A sauce made with egg yolks, butter, lemon juice and cayenne pepper.

Matelote: A fish soup or stew (generally made with freshwater fish), to which red or white wine and aromatics are added. It is covered and simmered gently over low heat.

Meunière: A method of cooking whole fish, steaks or fillets. The fish is lightly floured and sautéed in butter. During cooking the fish is sprinkled with lemon juice; it is then garnished with chopped parsley and the butter in which it was cooked, browned.

Miroton: A type of stew made by combining cooked meat or fish with sliced onions and lyonnaise sauce.

Tartar: A cold sauce served with fish. Based on mayonnaise prepared with a hard-boiled egg yolk and combined with capers, chopped sweet pickles, onions and fresh herbs.

Tempura: A Japanese method of preparing an assortment of foods, including seafood and small fish, which are quickly sautéed. The cooking is done at the table.

Conversion Chart

**Conversion Chart for the
Main Measures Used in
Cooking**

Volume		Weight	
1 teaspoon............	5 mL	2.2 lb.........	1 kg (1000 g)
1 tablespoon.........	15 mL	1.1 lb...............	500 g
		0.5 lb..............	225 g
1 quart (4 cups).......	1 litre	0.25 lb..............	115 g
1 pint (2 cups).......	500 mL		
1/2 cup............	125 mL		
1/4 cup............	50 mL	1 oz................	30 g

**Metric Equivalents
for Cooking
Temperatures**

49°C...............	120°F	120°C..............	250°F
54°C...............	130°F	135°C..............	275°F
60°C...............	140°F	150°C..............	300°F
66°C...............	150°F	160°C..............	325°F
71°C...............	160°F	180°C..............	350°F
77°C...............	170°F	190°C..............	375°F
82°C...............	180°F	200°C..............	400°F
93°C...............	200°F	220°C..............	425°F
107°C..............	225°F	230°C..............	450°F

Readers will note that, in the recipes, we give 250 mL as the equivalent for 1 cup and 450 g as the equivalent for 1 lb and that fractions of these measurements are even less mathematically accurate. The reason for this is that mathematically accurate conversions are just not practical in cooking. Your kitchen scales are simply not accurate enough to weigh 454 g—the true equivalent of 1 lb—and it would be a waste of time to try. The conversions given in this series, therefore, necessarily represent approximate equivalents, but they will still give excellent results in the kitchen. No problems should be encountered if you adhere to either metric or imperial measurements throughout a recipe.

Index